Managing Higher Education in Colleges

Managing Higher Education in Colleges

Gareth Parry, Anne Thompson and Penny Blackie

continuum

Continuum International Publishing Group

The Tower Building   80 Maiden Lane, Suite 704
11 York Road   New York
London SE1 7NX   NY 10038

British Library Cataloguing-in-Publication Data
A catalogue record for this book is available from the British Library.

ISBN: 0 8264 8846 3 (paperback)

Typeset by Fakenham Photosetting Limited, Fakenham, Norfolk
Printed and bound in Great Britain by MPG Books Ltd, Bodmin,
Cornwall

Contents

Acknowledgements

The authors would like to thank the following people for their advice and particularly for reading and commenting on chapters of the book:

Gay Bligh, Kevin Buckley, Hugh Butcher, Carol Gibson, Maggie Greenwood, Susan Hayday, Gillian Hayes, Russell Joseph, Margaret Lawson, Phil Lester, Philip Lloyd, Derek Longhurst, Stephanie Marshall, Russell Moseley, Colin Rainey, Bev Sand, Sarah Shobrook, Wendy Staples, Toby West-Taylor, Iain Wolloff.

The content of all parts of the book is, however, the responsibility of the authors.

Series foreword

THE ESSENTIAL FE TOOLKIT SERIES

Jill Jameson
Series Editor

In the autumn of 1974, a young woman newly arrived from Africa landed in Devon to embark on a new life in England. Having travelled half-way round the world, she still longed for sunny Zimbabwe. Not sure what career to follow, she took a part-time job teaching EFL to Finnish students. Enjoying this, she studied thereafter for a PGCE at the University of Nottingham in Ted Wragg's Education Dept. After teaching in secondary schools, she returned to university in Cambridge, and, having graduated, took a job in ILEA in 1984 in adult education. She loved it: there was something about adult education that woke her up, made her feel fully alive, newly aware of all the lifelong learning journeys being followed by so many students and staff around her. The adult community centre she worked in was a joyful place for diverse multi-ethnic communities. Everyone was cared for, including 90 year olds in wheelchairs, toddlers in the crèche, ESOL refugees, city accountants in business suits and university level graphic design students. In her eyes, the centre was an educational ideal, a remarkable place in which, gradually, everyone was helped to learn to be who they wanted to be. This was the Chequer Centre, Finsbury, ECI, the 'red house', as her daughter saw it, toddling in from the crèche. And so began the story of a long interest in further education that was to last for many years ... why, if they did such good work for so many, were FE centres so under-funded and unrecognized, so under-appreciated?

It is with delight that, 32 years after the above story began, I write the Foreword to *The Essential FE Toolkit*, Continuum's new book series of 24 books on further education (FE) for teachers and college leaders. The idea behind the *Toolkit* is to provide a comprehensive guide to FE in a series of compact, readable books. The suite of 24 individual books are gathered together to provide the practitioner with an overall FE toolkit in specialist, fact-filled volumes designed to be easily accessible, written by experts with significant knowledge and experience in their individual fields. All of the authors have in-depth understanding of further education. But '*Why is further education important? Why does it merit a whole series to be written about it?*' you may ask.

At the Association of Colleges Annual Conference in 2005, in a humorous speech to college principals, John Brennan said that, whereas in 1995 FE was a 'political backwater', by 2005 it had become 'mainstream'. John recalled that, since 1995, there had been '36 separate Government or Government-sponsored reports or white papers specifically devoted to the post-16 sector'. In our recent regional research report (2006) for the Learning and Skills Devlopment Agency, my co-author Yvonne Hillier and I noted that it was no longer 'raining policy' in FE, as we had described earlier (Hillier and Jameson, 2003): there is now a torrent of new initiatives. We thought, in 2003, that an umbrella would suffice to protect you. We'd now recommend buying a boat to navigate these choppy waters, as it looks as if John Brennan's 'mainstream' FE, combined with a tidal wave of government policies will soon lead to a flood of new interest in the sector, rather than end anytime soon.

There are good reasons for all this government attention on further education. In 2004/05, student numbers in LSC council-funded further education increased to 4.2 million, total college income was around £6.1 billion, and the average college had an annual turnover of £15 million. Further education has rapidly increased in national significance regarding the need for ever greater achievements in UK education and skills training for millions of learners, providing qualifications and workforce training to feed a UK national economy hungrily in competition with other OECD nations. The 120 recommendations of the Foster Review (2005) therefore in the main encourage colleges to focus their work on vocational skills, social inclusion and achieving academic progress. This series is here to consider all three of these areas and more.

The series is written for teaching practitioners, leaders and managers in the 572 FE/LSC-funded institutions in the UK, including FE colleges, adult education and sixth form institutions, prison education departments, training and workforce development units, local education authorities and community agencies. The series is also written for PGCE/Cert Ed/City & Guilds Initial and continuing professional development (CPD) teacher trainees in universities in the UK, USA, Canada, Australia, New Zealand and beyond. It will also be of interest to staff in the 600 Jobcentre Plus providers in the UK and to many private training organisations. All may find this series of use and interest in learning about FE educational practice in the 24 different areas of these specialist books from experts in the field.

Our use of this somewhat fuzzy term 'practitioners' includes staff in the FE/LSC-funded sector who engage in professional practice in governance, leadership, management, teaching, training, financial and administration services, student support services, ICT and MIS technical support, librarianship, learning resources, marketing, research and development, nursery and crèche services, community and business support, transport and estates management. It is also intended to include staff in a host of other FE services including work-related training, catering, outreach and specialist health, diagnostic additional learning support, pastoral and religious support for students. Updating staff in professional practice is critically important at a time of such continuing radical policy-driven change, and we are pleased to contribute to this nationally and internationally.

We are also privileged to have an exceptional range of authors writing for the series. Many of our series authors are renowned for their work in further education, having worked in the sector for 30 years or more. Some have received OBE or CBE honours, professorships, fellowships and awards for contributions they have made to further education. All have demonstrated a commitment to FE that makes their books come alive with a kind of wise guidance for the reader. Sometimes this is tinged with world-weariness, sometimes with sympathy, humour or excitement. Sometimes the books are just plain clever or a fascinating read, to guide practitioners of the future who will read these works. Together, the books make up a considerable portfolio of assets for you to take with you through your journeys in further education. We hope the experience of reading the books will be interesting, instructive and pleasurable and that experience gained from them will last, renewed, for many seasons.

It has been wonderful to work with all of the authors and with Continuum's UK Education Publisher, Alexandra Webster, on this series. The exhilarating opportunity of developing such a comprehensive toolkit of books probably comes once in a lifetime, if at all. I am privileged to have had this rare opportunity, and I thank the publishers, authors and other contributors to the series for making these books come to life with their fantastic contributions to FE.

Dr Jill Jameson
Series Editor
March, 2006

Series introduction

THE ESSENTIAL FE TOOLKIT SERIES

Jill Jameson
Series Editor

When I first proposed a publication on further education (FE) to Alexandra Webster at Continuum in autumn, 2003, I had one particular book in mind. This was envisaged as a book which would span a number of areas across the further and higher education (FE/HE) sectors, to outline, in new ways, the process of 'minding the gap' between the two sectors, notably in relation to issues of leadership, management and lifelong learning. My own background during 1987–2004 in senior management in a number of colleges, as a Director of Lifelong Learning at the University of Greenwich, with responsibility for HE–FE partnerships, lifelong learning and widening participation initiatives, meant that I was particularly interested in this area.

My early proposal for that one book developed into a much more extensive book series proposed during 2004 on FE, *The Essential FE Toolkit*, the initial focus of which was to provide a *Survival Guide* for lecturers, managers and teacher trainees in FE. The story of the development of the series is too detailed to report in full here. Suffice it to say that, as Alexandra and I worked for many hours discussing the proposed details of this major new book series, the question of 'minding the gap' between universities and further education institutions was never far from our minds. We felt that a specialist book providing an expert guide to the provision of higher education in further education was an essential part of the *Toolkit*. I said I knew the perfect authoring team for it! I am delighted to confirm that we successfully invited or preferred team of expert authors: Professor Gareth Parry, Dr Anne Thompson and Penny Blackie, three UK experts in the field, to write this timely book, *Managing Higher Education in Colleges*, which provides a vital contribution to the *Essential FE Toolkit*.

This authoritative guide on the management of HE provision in FE is written for managers in further education, including those in general, specialist and sixth form colleges, as well as staff and managers in universities and businesses who have key roles to play in supporting the provision of higher education in colleges. The book outlines and analyses different organisational structures, funding relationships, quality assurance and administration arrangements for the effective management, coordination and support of higher education qualifications and progression routes in colleges.

This includes the identification of diverse methods of strategic planning, organisation, curriculum delivery, funding and partnership for the successful provision of operational and quality support for higher education in colleges. The authors identify key tasks, checklists and procedures necessary at college level to provide effective higher education. They outline the arrangements for courses at undergraduate, post-graduate, diploma and certificate courses funded by HEFCE (the Higher Education Funding Council for England) and higher level qualifications funded by the LSC (Learning and Skills Council).

The management of higher education in colleges has increasingly gained importance in the UK and internationally during past decades. Since the Dearing Inquiry of 1996–7, there has been a growing emphasis on the need for higher level professional, vocational and advanced technical skills. This need has been communicated in several major UK government policy initiatives since 1997 that have been designed to stimulate the development of mass higher education, including policies and funding opportunities for widening participation (WP), Partnerships for Progression (P4P), New Technology Institutes (NTIs) and Lifelong Learning Networks (LLNs). Amongst the specialist qualifications on offer, Foundation Degree programmes have gathered momentum since their introduction in 2000–01, emphasising the role of colleges in delivering regional, well-supported opportunities for wider participation in higher education at sub-degree, undergraduate and advanced technical levels and above. Numbers of students studying at higher education levels currently comprise around one in nine of all UK HE students, and this figure is likely to grow rather than diminish.

The book provides an excellent overview of the recent past and current state of higher education in colleges in England, reflecting on current issues and trends arising from the implications of recent policy developments, including the 2006 White Paper on FE, the 'managed provider networks' concept and other recommendations form the Foster Review (2005) and recent developments and changes in QAA and HEFCE-led quality and partnership precepts, reviews and guidelines. The book is an admirably compact and helpful guide to support readers grappling with the enormous complexity of FE-delivered higher education provision. A perceptive analysis of current key issues and questions in the *Conclusion*, supplemented by excellent Appendices with detailed references, gives valuable advice for FE managers on current changes and future developments. This book is a 'must-read' for all those delivering and supporting higher education in colleges.

Dr Jill Jameson

Figures and tables

Introduction

Whether higher education is a small or large part of the work of further education colleges, the management and coordination of this activity is a matter of growing importance. Although their contribution to higher education is long-standing, it is only in recent years that colleges have been asked to play a more central role. In partnership with higher education institutions and employers, further education establishments are expected to deliver the new kinds of vocational higher education required by a high-skills economy. To pursue this part of their mission, they deal with organisations that fund higher education and that monitor its quality and standards. To secure a share of the student market, they compete as well as collaborate with universities and other institutions in the higher education sector. Whatever its scale, managing this activity is a serious undertaking.

Yet, higher education is always a minority of the work of further education colleges. In most cases it is small fraction of their provision. The priorities that govern the rest of their activity will invariably dominate the business of management or call for specific and separate attention. Among these are pressures on colleges to focus their mission. General further education colleges, where most of the higher education in the learning and skills sector is found, are pressed to cultivate a specialist vocational identity in one or more areas. In these circumstances, a more strategic approach to the management and development of higher education is required of colleges: one addressed to the integration and sustainability of such provision as well as its distinctiveness.

Least likely to develop a strategic view of their higher education are colleges with small pockets of activity. As ever, there is a risk of isolation and life on the periphery of the institution. All the same, courses can arise, evolve and do well in this context. Others survive, decline or fail to get started. Colleges with significant proportions of higher education will already have a clear strategy for work at these levels. New qualifications, subjects and modes can be added that complement those in further education and which provide a platform for growth. If the goal is to achieve a balance of higher and further education, then a more integrated model of management is likely to emerge. This is all the more strategic where the plan is to leave the sector altogether, through merger or by being designated a higher education institution.

This book is a guide to the management of higher education in all further education settings. In particular, we outline the key tasks and main issues posed by the development of programmes and qualifications at these levels. These settings include general, specialist and sixth-form colleges. In addition to undergraduate programmes funded directly or indirectly by the funding council for higher education, along with postgraduate courses occasionally taught in colleges, we also include higher-level qualifications supported in the learning and skills sector. The significance of the latter is that they are frequently regarded and managed differently from the rest of higher education in the same college.

Since managers in further education are the primary audience, much of the book is concerned with the expectations, procedures and requirements of organisations that support and regulate the programmes of higher education provided by further education colleges. Rather less is said about the systems and priorities that shape the way in which colleges deliver their further education, although we highlight the competing policies and parallel arrangements that arise from a division into two sectors. Our concern is with publicly funded programmes and qualifications, not those provided commercially by colleges and targeted, for example, at international students. That said, we recognise that the costs of publicly funded provision are shared directly with students and that distinctions between full-time and part-time study carry less meaning than previously.

Throughout the text, we try to represent this flux and diversity, drawing on examples in the literature and the experiences of the authors. We ourselves have occupied manager-practitioner-research positions within and between further and higher education. Two of us have been senior managers in colleges with contrasting amounts and types of higher education. The third has worked in both the college and university sectors. As analysts, developers and evaluators, we bring a range of perspectives to bear on the variety and complexity of this provision and its management. Our approach is to combine practical understanding with contextual commentary.

We have written in ways that should be useful to new and more experienced managers alike. Such individuals might have college-wide responsibilities, undertake coordinating roles, or lead the delivery of individual courses. In colleges with small amounts of higher education, the course or programme leader is sometimes the institutional focus for the management function. Where programmes are offered in association with other organisations, a partnership manager might oversee or share responsibility for higher level work. In some of the larger providers, there are members of the senior management team whose sole remit is higher education. Elsewhere, this remit might be included in the work of a senior manager whose other responsibilities are college-wide.

The book is also relevant to college personnel who need to know about specific aspects of this activity, such as its funding and quality assurance, its teaching, learning and widening participation strategies, and its marketing and information management. To this end, the chapters can be read independently or in combination. The text is useful as well to staff in higher education institutions, especially those with responsibility for relationships with further education. As a result of history or merger or transfer, a few higher education institutions have considerable amounts of work funded and inspected by agencies in the learning and skills sector. Similar to staff in the colleges, there will be those holding positions that go across higher and further education.

Like much else about college-based higher education, there is only a slim base of evidence to inform understanding about the organisation, management and conduct of this activity. This is especially so in England, the focus of our discussion. The English system is a rapidly changing one, with an array of reform measures and special initiatives bearing on the involvement and future commitment of colleges to higher education. This book is written immediately prior to the implementation of variable tuition fees and bursary schemes for full-time undergraduate education in England in 2006. We expect fee deregulation to bring more turbulence in higher education, especially if the upper limit on fee levels is raised or removed in the future. An early review of the new fee arrangements is scheduled for 2009.

This is one of a number of developments that will influence how higher education is undertaken in further education in the years to come. The report of the Foster review of further education colleges in England was published at the end of 2005. The government response to its recommendations took the form of a White Paper on further education in 2006, with major implications for the higher education and higher-level skills delivered in this sector. This included a strengthening of the role of colleges in providing higher education programmes linked to their economic and social mission.

Other changes are likely to follow an internal review of higher education in further education colleges carried out by the funding council for higher education, such as new codes of practice to replace those for franchise and consortia funding. If adopted, a new method of external quality review will bring directly and indirectly funded courses into a single process, with encouragement for colleges to manage and develop their higher education as an integrated whole. For its part, the funding council for the learning and skills sector developed, for the first time, its own higher education strategy.

Some things, however, are set to continue, at least for the time being. Unlike in Scotland, where the funding councils for further and higher education merged in 2005, policies in England presuppose the continuation of a two-sector system. Separate funding and quality regimes have proved no obstacle to the growth of cross-sector partnerships. Indeed, structured partnerships between universities, employers and colleges are the main vehicle for the Foundation degree. Much of the future expansion in under-graduate education is expected to come from this new qualification and colleges are accorded a central role in its delivery. By the end of the decade, the participation rate in higher education is intended to approach, if not reach, 50 per cent of the 18 to 30 age group.

Our account is for the period including the academic year 2005–06 and incorporating any known changes for 2006–07. While seeking to be up-to-date and authoritative, we signal themes, principles and questions likely to be of significance in the longer term. At the same time, we note the continuing difficulty faced by colleges in building a public and powerful argument for their involvement in higher education. In proposing that colleges evolve a strategy to better manage the size, shape and direction of their higher-level work, we make our own contribution to a larger argument for new configurations of higher and further education in the English system.

In Part One (Chapters 1 and 2), we examine the changing contexts for higher education in further education and the institutional patterns that have evolved. These are chapters that set the scene for a more detailed treatment of what features should be addressed in the day-to-day and strategic management of education at these higher levels. In this first section, we also engage with the often confusing and changing terminologies applied to this provision. In Part Two (Chapters 3 to 7), which is the core of the book, we have separate chapters on the organisation of this activity and the management of its funding, partnerships, quality and teaching. In Part Three (Chapter 8), we consider the strategic issues and options for colleges as they encounter uncertain, ambiguous and uneven conditions for their higher-level work.

Clarity, consistency and a minimum of overlap between chapters have been a common goal. Nevertheless, our individual authorship of chapters is reflected in somewhat different styles of writing. We have kept abbreviations and acronyms to a minimum. At the back of the book, we provide a guide to selected terminology, a summary of key funding initiatives and documents, and a list of relevant major organisations, including their publications and web addresses.

As apparent in the title of the book, one of the conventions we have chosen to follow is the use of 'college' or 'colleges' as a shorthand for establishments of further education. We justify this usage on two counts. First, there are now only a few non-university higher education institutions with the word 'college' in their title and most of these are specialist establishments. Second, colleges are the largest set of providers in the learning and skills sector and, for this reason, they are sometimes termed the 'college sector' or the 'college system'. Unlike in many official documents, we also prefer to describe all those enrolled in both sectors as 'students' rather than 'learners'.

1 Changing contexts, changing policies

What are the contexts to be managed by further education colleges engaging in higher education? How are they changing? What are the sources and directions of change? In this chapter, we trace some of the main movements in public policy over the recent period, especially those most likely to influence institutional behaviour and decision-making in the years ahead. In the following chapter, we examine the variety of higher education that is undertaken in the college system, including the ways it is described. Together, these chapters set the scene for a more detailed treatment in the rest of the book of the funding, quality and other relationships that are central to the management of higher education in further education settings.

At a time when policies on education and learning have proliferated, only a few are addressed directly or specifically to higher education in further education. There are other policies that have equal, or even greater, significance for the college role in higher education, but their main focus or purpose is elsewhere. What both sets of policy have in common is their origin and elaboration outside the learning and skills sector. Whether and how they engage in higher education is a matter for individual colleges and much less, if at all, for their sector bodies. Except for the higher-level work eligible for support within their own sector, colleges must look to organisations in the higher education sector for their main sources of policy, funding and monitoring.

Apart from broad policy statements from the Department for Education and Skills (DfES), it is largely through the requirements of the Higher Education Funding Council for England (HEFCE) and the Quality Assurance Agency for Higher Education (QAA) that the college contribution to higher education is steered, reviewed and, occasionally, articulated. This is an important but secondary part of the work of these agencies, in much the same way that higher education is a distinctive yet small segment in the work of most colleges.

As the primary funding and planning body for qualifications at the further education levels, the Learning and Skills Council (LSC) has no remit for higher education. However, it does have the power to fund vocational and professional qualifications at the higher levels. It also has an interest in qualifications and pathways that facilitate progression between further and higher education. This is the subject of a Joint Progression Strategy operated by HEFCE and the LSC (with the DfES). As in its collaboration with the Further Education Funding Council (FEFC), the predecessor to the LSC, the HEFCE is normally the lead partner.

These administrative, financial and regulatory frameworks encompass patterns of higher education that have evolved under different historical, geographical and political conditions. Some present-day colleges initially accepted students onto higher education courses as early as the 1950s. Others did not acquire their higher education until much later, during the dramatic expansion of the late 1980s and early 1990s, or in response to the new wave of policies that are the subject of this chapter. Whatever their particular origins, and however small their contribution, the colleges that now teach around one in nine of the students in English higher education are part of a long tradition of locally provided courses at these levels.

Here we highlight six key features of the contemporary policy environment that bear on how this provision is managed and developed:

- a new and enhanced role for colleges in higher education
- the preservation of sectors
- the drive to near-universal access
- the creation of a flagship qualification
- the rise of semi-compulsory partnerships
- more and deeper differentiation.

A new and enhanced role for colleges in higher education

Colleges perform two main roles in relation to higher education. They enable young people and adults to qualify for entry to higher education, mainly for admission to full-time programmes leading to honours degrees at higher education institutions (HEIs). Second, they themselves provide courses of undergraduate education, usually but not exclusively for short-cycle and vocationally oriented qualifications. Both roles are performed by the majority of colleges. Nevertheless, it is the 'qualifying' rather than the 'providing' function that is better known and more extensive.

Further education institutions in England contribute more than a third of entrants to higher education but only a minority of this cohort remain in the college (or join another in the same sector) to pursue their undergraduate studies. Those that stay in further education for their higher education, or join after a period away from the education system, generally follow part-time or full-time programmes leading to Higher National Certificate (HNC), Higher National Diploma (HND) and, since 2001, Foundation degree (Fd) qualifications. Many of these courses now increasingly offer progression to the honours level, sometimes within the college or by transfer to a degree-awarding institution.

Some of this higher education is taught on behalf of an HEI under a franchise or collaborative agreement. Franchising grew rapidly during the peak expansion years and continued at a reduced scale after 1994, when a cap was placed on numbers in full-time undergraduate education. Many of the former polytechnics had franchise relationships with several colleges and, as post-1992 universities, they still account for the majority of franchise students. Some colleges had collaborative arrangements with more than one HEI and many continue to do so.

Prior to 1997, much of this directly funded and franchised activity attracted little attention from the central authorities in either sector. At this time, HEFCE had funding responsibility for most undergraduate and nearly all postgraduate education (known formally as 'prescribed' higher education) and the FEFC funded the HNC and other courses providing education at the higher levels (otherwise referred to as 'non-prescribed' higher education).

The low levels of policy interest in college-based higher education reflected, in part, the smaller share and weaker demand for courses below the level of the honours degree as well as the dispersed and part-time character of much of the provision.

That policy profile changed with the publication of the report of an independent inquiry into the future development of higher education (the Dearing committee, 1996–97) and the acceptance by a newly elected Labour government of its recommendations on renewed growth. To the surprise of many commentators, the report recommended that future expansion should be focused on 'sub-degree' higher education and that further education colleges should be funded directly to take the majority of the growth at these levels.

We are keen to see directly funded sub-degree higher education develop as a special mission for further education colleges. In general, over time, we see much more of this level of provision being offered in these colleges, although we recognise that particular circumstances might apply in some cases. We also see no case for expanding degree or postgraduate work in further education colleges.

(NCIHE 1997: 260)

The recommendation was controversial on several fronts. First, it assumed that a large part of future growth would be expressed at the sub-degree levels. Second, it expected colleges to take the bulk of this expansion, even though they had been detached from non-university higher education in 1988 and incorporated in 1993 to fulfil a further education mission, unburdened by higher-level work. Third, the sub-degree higher education provided by further education was to be funded directly by HEFCE and not indirectly by the use of franchising (which in its multiple and serial forms was considered a threat to quality and standards). Finally, colleges were accorded a special mission at the sub-degree level that would distinguish their higher education from others and guard against any upward (academic) drift in their higher education role.

Any public debate on these matters was overtaken by the introduction of a flat-rate up-front tuition fee for full-time undergraduate education, including that offered in further education colleges, and by the replacement of maintenance grants by loans. This policy, announced by the newly elected Blair government in

1997, accepted the Dearing recommendation for a private contribution to the costs of tuition, but rejected the model of funding and
student support favoured by the inquiry. However, fees repayable
when in employment and student grants, two key elements in the
Dearing model, were to return in the new scheme for variable
tuition fees after 2006. As before, the measure applied to all full-
time undergraduate courses, irrespective of their location.

The preservation of sectors

In the event, none of the Dearing proposals on the special mission
for colleges was implemented in full. Rather than look only to
direct funding, HEFCE offered colleges a choice and combination
of funding options, including franchise and consortium arrangements. Not only was indirect funding accepted and established as
a normal funding route, it was actively encouraged by HEFCE,
especially where colleges taught small amounts of higher education
in isolation from other parts of the college curriculum.

As a result, the Dearing presumption that each college should
have only one higher education franchise partner was relaxed. In
parallel with the publication of codes of practice on indirectly
funded partnerships by HEFCE in 1999 and 2000, the QAA
produced its own code of practice on collaborative provision in
1999. A second edition of the QAA code was published in 2004
to incorporate a revision of the guidelines on distance learning.
The original HEFCE codes remained in place in 2005–06, but
were likely to be revised in the light of proposals for a new funding
method for teaching and a new quality review process for higher
education in colleges.

Following another Dearing proposal, responsibility for the
funding of all undergraduate and postgraduate education in
England passed to HEFCE. After 1999, the HNC was included
in the prescribed higher education funded by HEFCE. This left
the FEFC, and subsequently the LSC, responsible for funding an
assortment of vocational and professional programmes leading to
higher-level qualifications. Within this non-prescribed category
of higher education were courses undertaken in preparation for
professional examinations, along with a small collection of National
Vocational Qualifications (NVQs) at the higher levels.

The immediate result was to bring more than 260 colleges into direct funding by HEFCE, compared to just 70 or so colleges before this date. This number was gradually reduced as a result of colleges opting for indirect forms of funding. For some further education establishments, this was their first encounter with the HEFCE funding methodology and the subject-by-subject assessment of courses by the QAA. By contrast, the higher-level qualifications that remained the funding responsibility of the FEFC came under the normal inspection arrangements for the college sector.

The transfer of funding responsibility to HEFCE was confirmation of the commitment in England to a dual system of post-secondary education. For the government, there was no reason why cross-sector collaborations should not continue to grow and prosper, as they had done previously. In particular, it looked to stronger partnerships at the regional level to assist not just in extending participation and progression, but to work with employers to address their skills requirements. Unlike in Scotland, where the funding councils were eventually merged, the scale and complexity of the English system, it was argued, did not favour unitary arrangements.

The abolition of the FEFC in 2001 and the inclusion of further education institutions in a larger sector under the LSC and a network of 47 local learning and skills councils brought colleges into funding and planning relationships with a host of other post-16 providers. Among these are providers of workforce development and training, school sixth forms, and adult and community learning. According to the then Secretary of State, it represented the most significant and far-reaching reform ever enacted to post-16 learning in England. Less radical was its preservation of a division, formalised in the 1980s, between higher education institutions on the one side and establishments predominantly concerned with other levels and styles of post-compulsory education on the other.

In outlining this reform, two main justifications were given for maintaining this separation:

First, uniquely, higher education's contribution is international and national as well as regional and local. Although universities should be responsive to the needs of local employers and business, both to meet skills requirements and in the application of research, they also operate on a wider stage and require a different approach to funding. Second, one of the main aims in creating the new Council [LSC] is to bring order to an area which is overly complex, and where there are critical issues to address about coherence and the quality of provision. Including higher education would undermine this by complicating significantly the Council's remit and making that remit so broad as to be difficult to manage.

(DfEE 1999: 42)

Universities and colleges might have complementary roles in advancing the knowledge economy but, as this and other government statements made plain, the most urgent challenges lay in 14 to 19 learning and the skills agenda, rather than higher education. In the short term, at least, colleges involved in higher education would continue to deal with organisations in another sector.

The drive to near-universal access

Funded directly or indirectly, the important role of colleges in the delivery of higher education was signalled again in government policies and targets for the first decade of the new century. Most prominent and argued over was a target to increase participation in higher education to, or towards, 50 per cent of those aged 18 to 30 by 2010. By 2003–04, the relevant figure stood at 43 per cent. This was a different measure of participation than employed hitherto and it brought into scope those parts of higher education outside the traditional territory of the full-time honours degree. With nearly all those achieving two or more passes in A-level examinations moving into higher education, attention now turned to holders of vocational qualifications and the younger age groups already in employment.

Unlike schools and most HEIs, general further education colleges were often locations for vocational qualifications at both the secondary and higher education levels, and where prescribed and non-prescribed higher education could be found together. Although undergraduate education below the honours degree was a smaller proportion of higher education than previously, colleges now provided most of the HND and HNC courses in the English system.

At the same time, more and more students initially enrolled for short-cycle courses, the HND in particular, were choosing to complete their studies at degree level. Some colleges already possessed or were seeking to develop their own 'top-up' years. Elsewhere, students moved to a higher education establishment if they wished to join an honours programme. Often, those transferring to an HEI were required to undertake more than one further year of undergraduate study, depending on the match between the college course and honours degree.

The growing importance of the 'transfer' function, and different lengths of time to completion, raised questions for the government about the efficiency and equity of such arrangements. Offering higher education in college settings might, it was argued, prove attractive and accessible to the new types of student necessary to meet the 50 per cent target. It might also help broaden the social base of undergraduate education. Less acceptable was a role for colleges in undergraduate education that relieved the universities of their responsibility for widening participation or which promoted academic transfer at the expense of vocational and work-based higher education.

Despite its policy elevation, there were some, including those within the higher education sector, who queried the whole idea of higher education in further education. The cool reception given to some of the Dearing proposals on renewed growth reflected scepticism about whether demand in future years would favour qualifications below the honours level, especially if they were provided by further education institutions. Equally, there was unease about colleges assuming a special or exclusive role in the provision of the HND and HNC. The source of this general discomfort lay not just in the unequal status traditionally attached to university and non-university higher education but, more immediately, in the way that the English system acquired its 'mass' characteristics.

In contrast to Scotland, where higher national qualifications in the further education sector were a long-standing and substantial presence, the shift to a mass scale of higher education in England was accomplished without asking, expecting or needing colleges to take a leading role in this transition. In the English case, the spectacular expansion that saw a doubling of the full-time participation rate for young people, from 15 per cent in 1988 to around 30 per cent by 1994, was centred on the honours degree and the polytechnics and universities. Undergraduate education in the colleges was the slowest part of the system to expand and, without the teaching of franchised programmes, the proportion of higher education students studying in further education would have reduced.

With few signs of stronger demand for short-cycle qualifications such as the HND or HNC, the Blair government embarked on a series of measures that aimed to alter the shape of English higher education and 'break' the traditional pattern of demand for the undergraduate degree. In so doing, the economic and employer case for expansion was emphasised and the importance of quality and standards underlined:

But we do not believe that expansion should mean 'more of the same'. There is a danger of higher education becoming an automatic step in the chain of education, almost a third stage of compulsory schooling. We do not favour expansion on the single template of the traditional three-year honours degree.

Our overriding priority is to ensure that as we expand higher education places, we ensure that the expansion is of an appropriate quality and type to meet the demands of employers and the needs of the economy and students.

(DfES 2003a: 60)

The creation of a flagship qualification

The chosen vehicle for this steered expansion was the Foundation degree: a work-focused qualification awarded by HEIs, devised with employers and delivered 'typically' by colleges. First announced in 2000, the new qualification was intended to meet the shortage of people with technician level qualifications, develop in students the 'right' blend of skills needed by employers, and lay the basis for widening participation and progression. Offered in full-time (generally two years), part-time and mixed modes, it was aimed at those in work wanting to upgrade their skills (or change their occupation) as well as young people seeking vocational routes on leaving school or college.

Among the characteristics that distinguished this qualification from others were the close involvement of employers in the design and delivery of the curriculum, and a core role for work-based learning, including its integration with academic study and formal assessment. These were originally set out by HEFCE in its Foundation degree 'prospectus' and subsequently by QAA in the Foundation Degree Qualification Benchmark (FDQB). Progress in developing and delivering these design features was reviewed by QAA in 2002–03 and 2004–05, and by a Task Force that reported to ministers in 2004.

Alongside the opportunity for students to apply their learning to specific workplace situations, the same qualification was expected to afford smooth progression to the honours degree. To support academic transfer and secure its standing in the labour market, the Foundation degree could only be awarded by institutions with degree-awarding powers. In England, this was the first time that a short-cycle under-graduate qualification was given the title of 'degree'. It was also the first new major qualification in English higher education since the introduction of the Diploma of Higher Education (DipHE) in the 1970s. Moreover, by taking the bulk of future expansion in under-graduate education, the new degree was expected to subsume many of the other qualifications at these levels.

By the time of the 2003 White Paper on higher education, attention had turned to recognising Foundation degrees as 'ends in their own right'. While they remained part of a ladder of progression, the earlier requirements governing guaranteed progression were relaxed. Hereafter, Foundation degrees were officially described as 'employer-focused degrees that offer specific job-related skills'. With occupations at the associate professional and higher technician level expected to experience the greatest growth in the coming years, the urgent priority of government was to secure their reputation and extend their coverage to different sectors of employment.

The same White Paper announced the establishment of a dedicated national network – Foundation Degree Forward (Fdf) – to support the development and validation of high-quality Foundation degrees and so broker the next phase of expansion. Some colleges had argued for a national validation body, along the lines of the former Council for National Academic Awards (CNAA), which would have reduced their dependency on individual universities for validation services. The Fdf began its work in 2004, promoting the development of Foundation degrees, liaising with employers, Sector Skills Councils and regional bodies, gathering and disseminating good practice and offering advice on validation.

The investment in Foundation degrees anticipated a continuing, growing and changing role for colleges in higher education. On the other hand, the 'step-change' required in the quality and reputation of work-focused higher education brought a preferred model of funding and partnership to structure their delivery of Foundation degrees.

Further education colleges already play an important role in delivering higher education: they currently deliver 11 per cent of higher education. The vast majority of this (around 90 per cent) comprises two-year work-focused programmes, including Foundation degrees, which means that delivery through further education will be especially important as we reshape the pattern of expansion.

Further education has strengths in providing ladders of progression for students, particularly for those pursuing vocational routes, and serves the needs of part-time students and those who want to study locally. Further education colleges make an important contribution to meeting local and regional skills, including through the higher education they provide. We want this significant role to continue and to grow. However, it will be important that any expanded provision is of the high quality that we expect from higher education. We believe that structured partnerships between colleges and universities – franchise or consortium arrangements with colleges funded through partner HEIs – will be the primary vehicles to meet these aims and will deliver the best benefits for learners.

However, there will be some instances, such as where 'niche' provision is delivered or where there are no obvious partners, where direct funding of higher education in further education colleges may be more appropriate. These will be considered on a case-by-case basis by HEFCE, against criteria which include critical mass, track record on quality and standards, and nature of provision. HEFCE will issue new guidelines on the supply of places and funding of provision through colleges.

(DfES 2003b: 62)

The shift in favour of indirect funding and, with it, the need for colleges to enter into 'structured partnerships' with validating universities to expand their undergraduate work, were measures making for greater uncertainty in the management of higher education in the learning and skills sector.

In advance of variable fees, the 2003 White Paper intended to 'incentivise' both the supply of and demand for Foundation degrees. For institutions, it offered to fund additional places for Foundation degrees in preference to honours degree courses and to provide development funding for HEIs, colleges and employers to work together in designing more new Foundation degree courses. For students, it proposed bursaries for those doing Foundation degrees that could be used either for extra maintenance or to offset the fee for the course. While funds for growth and development have been allocated, including a 10 per cent premium to support the costs of partnership and a non-traditional student cohort, incentives on the demand side have not been applied.

The rise of semi-compulsory partnerships

Structured partnerships were the latest in a line of measures favouring indirect forms of funding. Not all colleges shared the same enthusiasm for such arrangements, especially if access to directly funded numbers was correspondingly reduced or denied altogether. Direct funding, it was claimed, made for a measure of independence and ownership not available to colleges in indirect funding relationships. While further education colleges had always to turn to a degree-awarding institution (such as a university) or an examination body (such as Edexcel) to validate, accredit and award their higher education qualifications, colleges in receipt of directly funded numbers were able to negotiate and pay for these services from their own purse. Even so, there was still a question about where ownership was located. In part, this was also a 'cultural' issue:

The staff who are perceived to 'own' the Foundation degree, having designed and developed it, are better motivated than staff who 'receive' the curriculum and pedagogy as given, and are asked just to deliver it. This difference in ownership perception can occur between different staff in the same institution. However, it is potentially more likely to occur in partnership arrangements where there is a dominant partner, usually the higher education institution. The obvious answer is to ensure that partnerships are genuine, and in particular that further education institutions are treated as full partners in design, development and delivery. There are good examples on which to build.

(DfES 2004: 23)

Most indirect funding partnerships took the form of franchise arrangements where agreement was reached on what funds were passed to the college for the supply of teaching and, in turn, what services were provided by the HEI. In franchise partnerships, as the HEFCE code of practice made plain, it was the HEI in receipt of council funding that was 'fully responsible' for the students and accountable for 'all aspects' of finance, administration and quality. This was not the case in the small number of HEFCE-recognised funding consortia, where funds were channelled through a lead institution (which might be an HEI or a college).

Unlike in funding consortia, there was wide variation in the proportion of funds retained by the HEI in franchise partnerships. The level of the top-slice was sometimes contentious. Where partnerships were well established, disagreements were few and usually resolved speedily and amicably. In other cases, however, acquiescence rather than agreement was the norm, often accompanied by an undercurrent of complaint. Again, there were concerns on both sides about how the costs of services were determined:

Many FECs were unclear as to how the figure was calculated and what was provided by the HEI in return. HEIs admitted to some difficulty in accurately costing the services they provided but, nonetheless, believed that the proportion of the funding retained did not cover their costs.

(HEFCE 2003a: 4)

Whatever their circumstances, structured partnerships for the delivery of higher education in further education were a widespread feature of the English system. Around half of higher education establishments and some two-thirds of further education colleges were party to indirect funding agreements, with the great majority of these relating to franchises and the remainder to HEFCE recognised consortia.

Moreover, partnerships that supported the 'providing' role of higher education in colleges intersected with a whole range of other collaborative activities aimed at increasing access, extending participation and building progression across the two sectors. Before the polytechnics and higher education colleges were removed from the local authority system in 1989, links between these institutions and those colleges mainly concerned with 'non-advanced' further education were promoted by local authorities, especially in the large metropolitan areas. Many of these early collaborations, including linked access courses, formed the basis for the franchise relationships that developed during the expansion years.

In the post-Dearing period, joint funding by HEFCE and the FEFC was used to foster widening participation partnerships between institutions in each sector and, more specifically, to encourage the development of progression opportunities from further to higher education. Two other features accompanied this movement: first, an increasing emphasis on the regional and sub-regional dimensions of cross-sector working; and second, a growing preoccupation with vocational progression and employer-focused higher education.

Following the creation of the LSC, these activities were styled Partnerships for Progression (P4P) and, at one stage, led to ambitious proposals for collaborative work between schools, colleges, employers and HEIs. In 2004, P4P was brought together with Excellence Challenge into the national Aimhigher programme. Together with the DfES, the funding councils for higher and post-16 education have developed a Joint Progression Strategy to advance vocational and workplace progression into and through higher education.

As part of this strategy, development funding and additional student numbers were used to create Lifelong Learning Networks (LLNs). Operating across a city, area, region or subject, and combining the strengths of a number of diverse institutions, these networks of (mainly) higher and further education providers were expected to bring greater clarity, coherence and certainty to progression opportunities for vocational students.

More and deeper differentiation

Recent policies directed at higher and further education have, as one of their primary aims, the greater differentiation of the system by sector, provider, programme and qualification to increase participation and achievement by young people and adults as well as meet the needs of employers and the economy. Furthermore, governments have been prepared to use both the market and central intervention to 'deliver' these objectives.

In higher education, measures directed at differentiation and diversification have included the launch of the Foundation degree, increased selectivity in the allocation of research funds, and the introduction of variable tuition fees. The government would continue to be the main source of funding for teaching and research and knowledge transfer but, in future, institutions should have 'greater freedom' to access new funding sources on their own account. Alongside deregulation has come new regulation, as in the requirement for all institutions to have an access agreement approved by the Office for Fair Access (Offa) before they could raise the level of tuition fee.

Similarly, efforts have been made to protect opportunities for vocational progression ahead of increased turbulence in the market for students and their fees. Since fewer choices were available to students on vocational programmes than for those on academic routes, there were worries that variable fees might exacerbate the problem:

Research-intensive universities may be persuaded to withdraw from the limited progression arrangements that they currently operate, while competition intensifies between some higher education institutions and further education colleges in the provision of vocational progression. More intense competition might, perversely, operate to restrict opportunity to fewer institutions and programmes, and confine those that do progress to relatively narrow pathways.

(HEFCE 2004: 4)

By inviting institutions to 'play to their strengths' within Lifelong Learning Networks, such configurations might help counter or ameliorate some of the distorting effects of competition:

As a more differentiated sector emerges, it remains important that the whole range of educational opportunity is available to learners as their lifetime needs, interests and abilities develop. LLNs will reconnect the sector where this meets the needs of learners, making the strengths of a more diverse sector readily accessible to them.' (ibid.: 4–5)

In further education, differentiation policies have been just as powerful and pervasive. As a result of the establishment of the learning and skills sector, a combination of competition, collaboration and strategic area review was expected to produce clearer differentiation between providers, especially among the general further education colleges. To encourage the latter along this path, each was urged to play to their particular strengths and gain recognition as Centres of Vocational Excellence (CoVEs). By 2005, over half of general further education colleges had established at least one vocational specialism for which they were regarded as a centre of excellence locally, regionally or nationally.

In the same year, the government announced its intention to establish National Skills Academies in each of the major sectors of the economy. Led by employers, linked to the relevant Sector Skills Council and based on a hub-and-spoke model, they would collaborate with CoVEs and specialist schools to tackle skills shortages in their sector. The first four Academies were approved in 2005 and, although still surrounded by a fair amount of uncertainty, the longer-term aim was for at least another 12.

Alongside CoVE and Academy developments, general further education colleges were urged to nurture and designate 'distinct' provision to better support the learning of students on different types and levels of programme. In some cases, colleges had already established separate sixth-form centres for (mainly) A-level teaching, and higher education centres or campuses for their undergraduate work. Similar pressures were likely to lead to dedicated provision for the increased numbers of 14 to 16-year-olds in schools being taught in colleges under the Increased Flexibility Programme.

That a college might be offering vocational programmes to 14-year-olds in the compulsory system at the same time as delivering undergraduate courses in the higher education system highlighted the overlap in responsibilities and accretion of roles that the Foster review of further education colleges was asked to consider. The report on the review proposed that skills, 'an economic mission', should become the primary purpose of the further education college of the future. Building vocational skills for the economy, it asserted, was the tradition from which much of further education developed but which had been diluted in recent years.

A focus on vocational skills building is not a residual choice but a vital building block in the UK's platform for future prosperity. It gives FE colleges an unequivocal mission and the basis of a renewed and powerful brand image.

(Foster 2005: 16)

A primary focus on skills did not exclude or invalidate the other 'pillars' of social inclusion and academic progress. On the contrary, an emphasis on skills would itself 'turn out to be a huge driver' for social inclusion and improved personal self-esteem.

Throughout the report, the need and search for differentiation and specialisation was paramount. For general further education and tertiary colleges, there should be a stronger push, supported by incentives, to develop vocational specialisms, and these should be connected by hub-and-spoke arrangements embracing the new Skills Academies and a revised CoVE programme. Sixth-form colleges, on the other hand, should retain their primary focus on academic achievement and progression for 16 to 19-year-olds and be treated as 'a distinctive institutional model'. Not only should their results be treated separately in official statistics but, within the DfES and the LSC, a stronger managerial focus on their role and contribution would be expected to lead to 'the removal of any barriers to market entry for new sixth-form colleges'.

Significantly, it was at the higher-levels in particular that further education colleges had a central role in the renewal and replenishment of skills.

The contribution of colleges to both progression and delivery of higher-level skills is absolutely essential, but this role is not widely recognised. This is absolutely central to the renewed skills purpose we propose in this report.

In addition:

FE colleges in England contribute more than a third of undergraduate entrants to higher education (indeed they are the main route for adults and for entrants from lower socio-economic groups). They are absolutely essential to the government's drive on widening participation in higher education. We must continue to bring down the walls between FE colleges and universities if we are to open such opportunities to everyone.' (ibid.: 19)

As before, collaborative partnerships between higher and further education institutions were seen as key to widening participation and supporting vocational progression in and through higher education, especially the 30 or so LLNs currently at various stages of development. In recommending that the government articulate a core role for general further education colleges in supplying economically valuable skills, HEFCE and the LSC, and the universities and the colleges, were asked again to work collaboratively to 'ensure clear learner pathways exist across the country to enable progression to higher levels'.

This and each of the other main Foster recommendations were accepted by the Blair government in the 2006 White Paper on further education. Significantly, the White Paper went much further than the Foster review in suggesting that the college role will 'continue to grow in importance' and that this should be linked to both the economic 'and' social mission of colleges. In line with the economic mission:

> there should be a presumption that HE delivered in FE should have a strong occupational and employment purpose. The major area of expansion will be Foundation degrees. We will also expand work-based HE programmes.

In accord with the social mission, the HEFCE is asked to treat widening participation, as well as employability, as high priorities for funding allocations:

> FE is particularly effective in providing HE for learners from more disadvantaged groups, backgrounds and communities. Many FE colleges offer flexible, local opportunities which make HE accessible to people who might otherwise face significant barriers to participation. This sector is well placed to promote wider participation in HE.
>
> (DfES 2006: 30)

However, not all colleges are considered well placed to provide higher education and those 'not delivering to the right standard' should not continue with work at this level. In another move aimed at differentiation, the White Paper proposed to prioritise the development of some larger college providers as 'centres of HE excellence' on the one side and to review the effectiveness of small pockets of provision on the other. Where access to higher education institutions is limited, the college role in higher education in regions is deemed particularly important, with new LLNs targeted at areas where provision is currently most sparse. Along with training providers, colleges are also the focus of new proposals within the Train to Gain framework to offer integrated training programmes for, and co-financed with, employers (from basic skills to higher education).

To support these developments, the HEFCE and the LSC were invited to explore mechanisms for further capital support to enable college providers to contribute to higher education. This included direct funding of higher education facilities in further education colleges and, importantly, another look at how individual programmes are presently funded. As well as investigation of small pockets of higher education activity, the two funding councils are charged to:

Review the financial arrangements that underpin HE courses in FE colleges, including franchising arrangements. It is important that money should follow the learner in ways that are transparent and build confidence. (ibid.: 31)

A guide to many of the organisations, initiatives and documents mentioned in this and other chapters can be found in each of the appendices at the end of the book.

2 Overlapping boundaries, diverse patterns

The policy and contextual changes described in the previous chapter have produced a diverse pattern of higher education in the learning and skills sector. Colleges differ not only in the size of this activity, but in the range of relationships, internal and external, necessary to support and secure this endeavour. How this provision is organised and where responsibility for its management is located will vary college by college, as we indicate in the next chapter.

Here, we highlight four features of this diversity:

- its scale and spread
- the mix of programmes
- the character of partnerships
- its claims to difference and distinctiveness.

We also consider some of the trends and movements making for greater complexity. Although our book is mainly concerned with management, coordination and strategy at the college level, an appreciation of larger and longer trends will help institutions position their programmes and define strategic priorities.

Terminological legacies and arrivals

Before commenting on these patterns, we review some of the terms employed to describe higher education in the learning and skills sector. In this book, we have adopted a broad definition of this territory to include courses of higher education funded directly or indirectly by HEFCE and programmes leading to higher level qualifications supported by the LSC. In legislation, this distinction is based on a schedule of courses eligible for funding from the higher education funding body. Those that attract grants from HEFCE are 'prescribed courses of higher education'. Those not eligible for funding from this body are other courses providing education 'at a higher level'.

In the old coinage, as well as conventionally, a course is at a higher level if its standard is above that of examinations at A-level or their recognised equivalents. In the new language of national qualification levels, higher education and higher level qualifications begin at level 4. Administratively, the application of these definitions has rarely been questioned. There has been less agreement about what this higher level provision should be called. For some, everything above A-level or level 3 should be regarded as higher education, whether it is prescribed or non-prescribed, or whether it is academic or vocational in orientation. For others, that described as higher education should be reserved for prescribed courses funded by HEFCE and separated from provision leading to higher level qualifications supported by the LSC.

The matter is well illustrated by the journey taken by the HNC during the 1980s and 1990s. Before 1989, this and all other higher education courses in the local authority system were funded as advanced further education. After that date, the HNC was not included among the courses of higher education prescribed for funding by the Polytechnics and Colleges Funding Council (PCFC) and then by HEFCE. Not on the prescribed list, its funding continued through the local authorities and then by the FEFC. In 1998, it joined the prescribed category and was added to the qualifications funded by HEFCE.

In the previous chapter, we noted the impact of this transfer of funding responsibility from the FEFC to HEFCE, both on the colleges that provided the HNC and the higher education agencies required thereafter to fund and review the quality and standards of these programmes. Discussions have since taken place about the possibility of other non-prescribed programmes being funded by HEFCE. The current review of the funding method for teaching in higher education has highlighted other issues linked to the regulations on prescribed provision, including restrictions on what amounts and levels of higher education can be funded directly by HEFCE in further education colleges. Whereas HEIs can be funded for small units of provision at all qualification levels, the funding of higher education in colleges is for courses of specified titles and types, as on the prescribed list.

There are further examples where the survival of old categories and the arrival of new nomenclatures make for ambiguity and occasional confusion. It is only in the recent period that national qualification frameworks have been developed to describe the levels at which major qualifications could or should be placed. Indeed, it was only in 2004 that the levels of the National Qualifications Framework (NQF), managed by the Qualifications and Curriculum Authority (QCA), were aligned to the Framework of Higher Education Qualifications (FHEQ) produced by the QAA for England, Wales and Northern Ireland. The alignment is shown in Appendix A, where we provide a guide to these and other key terms relevant to higher education in further education.

Here, we simply point to the potential for confusion that can arise when the numbering in the revised NQF (entry to level 8) is used alongside the different numbering (levels 1 to 4) and additional lettering (C, I, H, M and D) continued in the FHEQ. In the remainder of the book, we have adopted the following convention to distinguish between the higher level work in colleges funded by HEFCE (directly or indirectly) and that funded by the LSC. For the prescribed higher education supported by HEFCE, we use the FHEQ levels of certificate, intermediate, honours, masters and doctoral. For other education leading to qualifications at the higher levels (the non-prescribed category supported by the LSC), we use the NQF numerical levels (4 to 8).

When the Dearing inquiry made its recommendations on higher education in 1997, it described courses and qualifications below the honours degree as 'sub-degree' higher education. Historically, this reflected the dominance of the first degree in the English system and a tendency to equate undergraduate education with the first degree. It was not common to refer to 'other' levels of undergraduate education. Rather, these were collapsed, somewhat negatively, into 'non-degree' or 'sub-degree' higher education.

This old vocabulary has gradually been replaced by the FHEQ levels for undergraduate education and their main qualification titles: certificate (for Certificates of Higher Education); inter-mediate (for Foundation degrees, ordinary Bachelor's degrees, Diplomas of Higher Education and other higher diplomas); and honours (Bachelor's degrees with honours, Graduate Certificates and Graduate Diplomas). In practice, most such levels represent bands of qualifications sharing similar outcomes and those identified in the FHEQ cover the great majority of existing qualifications. One qualification not represented is the HNC. Its position in the framework could vary depending on the nature of the individual programme. Unlike the main qualification titles represented in the FHEQ, there are no qualification descriptors for this award.

The FHEQ and the revised NQF are qualification frameworks, not credit frameworks. Following the 2003 White Paper on Skills, the QCA was asked to lead the development of a unit-based qualification framework underpinned by a system of credit accumulation and transfer. The proposed Framework for Achievement (FfA) was designed to recognise 'a wider range of learner achievements' than the NQF. Tests and trials of the key features of the credit and qualifications framework, including that at the higher education levels, are scheduled for 2006 to 2008. At present, a number of universities and colleges participate in regional credit frameworks, which operate an agreed system for assigning and awarding credit.

Finally, we address another shift in language. Up to now, the term 'mixed economy' has been applied almost exclusively to a number of the largest providers of higher education in further education. The 'mixed economy group' (MEG) of colleges came together to represent their shared characteristics and interests to the sector bodies, especially those in higher education. By styling themselves in this fashion, they signalled their difference from other colleges and so sought different or separate treatment by the central authorities. Within government, the same terminology, 'mixed economy institution' (MEI), is beginning to be used for all colleges that have higher education and for all HEIs that offer further education, irrespective of the size of these shares. This usage is parallel to the concept of 'dual-sector' organization employed by some academic analysts and adopted in same national systems, such as Australia's.

Sizeable segments, small pockets

Which terminology is adopted, and how it is defined or interpreted, will influence what is included and counted as higher education in the learning and skills sector. In the rest of this chapter, we apply our broad definition of higher level education to examine the size, shape and pattern of development of undergraduate, postgraduate and higher level qualifications in further education in England. Assembling data on higher education in further education is a tricky exercise, partly because of the need to combine different datasets and partly because students might be taught in a different institution from that in which they are registered (as, for example, under franchise arrangements). Care should be taken therefore in comprehending and interpreting such information.

In the fifteen or so years since the breakthrough to mass higher education, the share of this work taken by colleges has changed very little. By contrast, patterns of higher education within and between colleges have assumed new shapes and directions. An estimated one in nine students undertake their higher education in further education and, significantly, the majority of these are concentrated in a minority of colleges. The rest populate the small pockets of higher education found in most general and specialist further education colleges and in a few sixth-form colleges.

At the point that the LSC assumed funding responsibility for most of the work of further education colleges, something like 190,000 higher education students were taught in more than 300 colleges (Parry, Davies and Williams 2003). Fewer than 60 establishments were responsible for half the total studying at these levels. Most (around two-thirds) were part-time students, with the HNC and higher level professional and technical qualifications accounting for nearly all the part-time activity. The third of students that were full-time were studying mainly for the HND, followed by a smaller proportion pursuing an honours degree.

In terms of funding, two-thirds of students were taught on programmes funded directly or indirectly by HEFCE: of these 6 per cent on postgraduate courses; 20 per cent on first-degree programmes; and 74 per cent on courses at the other undergraduate levels (the great majority studying for the HND and HNC, with roughly equal numbers on each). The other third of students were enrolled on programmes supported by the LSC: two-thirds on courses leading to higher level professional and technical qualifications; and a third working towards NVQs at levels 4 and 5. The significance of these categories and numbers is that, if a narrow definition were adopted which excluded the non-prescribed category funded by the LSC, then the college component of higher education would reduce to around 125,000. Without the LSC portion, the part-time proportion would fall considerably, although still a (slim) majority of the total population.

These were dimensions of higher education in further education into which the Foundation degree was launched in 2001. This began with the approval of 40 prototype programmes and a competition for additional student numbers (ASNs) for Foundation degree places. By 2005–06, there were 47,000 students on Fds, with slightly more studying full-time than part-time. There were roughly equal numbers on programmes based in HEIs as on courses delivered by colleges. Most of the latter provision was funded indirectly, predominantly through franchise partnerships.

Much of the impetus for this growth has continued to come from additional student numbers provided exclusively for this qualification. Some has also come from the conversion of higher national diplomas and certificates into Fds. The conversion of HNDs into Fds was the subject of one of three reports by the QAA that surveyed and reviewed this early phase of activity. Although the 2003 White Paper on higher education anticipated 'the integration of HNDs and HNCs into the Foundation degree framework' over this period, there remain a considerable number of higher national qualifications that retain their titles.

Combinations of programmes and qualifications

Whatever the method of counting, or the growth of Fd numbers, there is no alteration to the overall pattern of large amounts of higher education in just a handful of colleges and generally small pockets of provision in the remainder. All the same, these are aggregated numbers. While they assist management and planning at the system level, they offer little guide to what is offered by individual colleges.

Within colleges, there is no simple or common pattern of provision. Prescribed and non-prescribed, direct and indirect, and full-time and part-time higher education is found in different combinations in each institution. From the way that individual programmes are funded, validated and accredited will flow the reporting and quality assurance arrangements they are required to follow. Moreover, the significance attached to these categories and combinations will change over time. Accordingly, where and how the college management of these courses (and their partnerships) is conducted will differ in place and time, as we discuss in Chapter 3.

Just how varied the pattern is within and between colleges has been reported in recent studies undertaken for the Learning and Skills Development Agency (LSDA) and HEFCE. These and other relevant sources are listed in Appendices B and C. Even among the 20 largest and most long-standing providers of higher education, where direct funding of prescribed provision might be expected to dominate, there are examples of colleges with large proportions of franchised and non-prescribed provision. Among the same group, the balance between different levels of provision is far from regular, although nearly all have courses represented at the first degree, other undergraduate, postgraduate and other higher levels (Parry, Davies and Williams 2004).

These institutional profiles predate the growth of Foundation degrees. Given that around one in three students are studying on Fds delivered through indirect funding partnerships, this might have added to the number and proportion of franchise students in individual colleges. It is difficult, however, to assess the impact of this new qualification when colleges are converting some of their provision to Foundation degrees, or moving from direct to indirect funding, or gaining their own numbers in other ways, such as through Lifelong Learning Networks (LLNs).

Across the three main types of higher education in further education – prescribed direct, prescribed indirect and non-prescribed – the shift to indirect funding is the most dynamic element in this environment. Looking back, one of the key movements influencing the contemporary pattern of higher education in further education has been the sub-contracting of undergraduate teaching to colleges by partner HEIs. Franchising, as it was then called, first came to prominence during the years of mass expansion. With it came a more distributed system of higher education. Some colleges were brought into higher education for the first time. Others diversified their higher education, extending the range of subjects, levels and qualifications taught in the locality or region.

By the turn of the century, franchise students accounted for 30 per cent of all those taught on courses of prescribed higher education in the colleges. Given slack demand for higher education in the post-Dearing years, especially for HNDs and HNCs, franchising was a means by which the post-16 sector was able to maintain rather than increase its share of higher education. Franchise arrangements brought students into colleges at each of the undergraduate levels (along with a few at the postgraduate levels) and their numbers included a higher proportion of full-time students than those registered by colleges on their directly funded higher education courses. At the same time, franchising contributed to the instability and uncertainty of higher education in further education settings, with numbers able to be expanded, contracted or withdrawn at the discretion of the higher education institution.

In contrast to franchising and other forms of collaborative provision, the non-prescribed programmes offered by colleges have been largely hidden from policy. Until recently, such provision was rarely mentioned or reported. Three parallel developments have brought these qualifications to the attention of the government. One was the establishment of the National Qualifications Framework. As a condition of continued public funding, these qualifications had to be accredited by the regulatory bodies for inclusion in the NQF. Another was the 50 per cent target for participation in higher education which, in the search for new student numbers, prompted a closer look at the whole territory of higher level vocational and work-based education. Both exercises found an expression in a third and more wide-ranging enterprise: a government strategy on skills outlined in two White Papers (2003 and 2005) and informed by a major review of the future skills base for the UK (Leitch Review, 2005–06).

Inside colleges, the response to the higher level skills part of this strategy was frequently more evident in the activities around Foundation degrees than in developments pertaining to non-prescribed higher education. This unevenness was commonly reflected in the management of these two domains. Courses funded directly or indirectly by HEFCE tended to be viewed, if not always managed, in common. Higher level programmes preparing students for specific and specialist examinations, or providing continuing professional development, were often distributed across different departments and regarded neither as a whole nor as higher education.

Partnerships and other collaborations

As colleges look more and more to degree-awarding institutions for resources and services, so the management of their higher education is increasingly concerned with the negotiation, operation and review of partnerships. In some settings, this might be no more than a single or part-programme delivered on behalf of one HEI. Elsewhere, this might extend to a whole range of collaboratively taught provision where one or a number of HEIs have indirect funding agreements with an individual college. Where the same college has directly funded provision, one or more other awarding bodies might have partnership agreements to provide validation and quality assurance services.

In their design or delivery or both, some courses – Foundation degrees in particular – will involve formal collaboration with employers, the local chambers of commerce, the Sector Skills Councils and the regional development agencies. Programmes and projects at other levels of education in the college might have similar groups in partnership and, commonly, will overlap and intersect with those addressed to higher education. The proliferation of partnerships across many areas of the curriculum has led some colleges to identify a senior manager to coordinate this activity. Where there are multiple partnerships underpinning the higher level work of the college, the management of these relationships might rest with a higher education coordinator.

Like the history of directly funded higher education in a college, many present-day partnerships have their origin in earlier access collaborations and in later regional and sub-regional engagements, including those benefiting from development funds distributed jointly by HEFCE and the LSC. As competition for students has intensified, colleges find themselves courted more regularly by HEIs seeking to meet their target numbers or win additional funded places. For their part, colleges are becoming more strategic in their decisions about whether to move from one organisation to another to secure a better 'deal' for the teaching they provide for HEIs or the validation they require for their own programmes.

In many ways, the switch in government policy away from direct funding of undergraduate education in colleges has revived the market for indirect funding partnerships. Compared to earlier years, when few controls were placed on the pattern of franchise activity, structured partnerships between colleges and HEIs are now guided by government policy and overseen by the funding and quality bodies. Most funding partnerships continue to take the form of franchise arrangements where agreement is reached on the funds passed to the college for the supply of teaching in return for the quality assurance and other functions performed by the HEI.

There is no monitoring of these agreements beyond the codes of practice issued by HEFCE and the QAA. Franchise agreements are first and foremost legal and commercial contracts, although some make reference to principles and practices of collaboration. Only in the case of HEFCE-recognised funding consortia, where funds are channelled through a lead institution, did the funding council have sight of the underpinning contract. In a franchise partnership, the HEI is formally responsible and accountable for all that is undertaken in its name, including the quality of the experience made available to students. As the HEFCE code of practice acknowledged, this necessarily implied a hierarchical relationship between the two parties. Consortia agreements, on the other hand, gave more recognition to colleges as equal partners and allowed for a further education establishment to be the lead institution.

Notwithstanding this mix of competition and regulation, franchise partnerships have multiplied, diversified and, where in existence for a considerable time, been able to establish relationships of confidence and trust. One important source of variation in these partnerships is the amount of funding retained by the HEI in an indirect funding agreement. A recent review of these arrangements found colleges reporting top slices ranging from 8 per cent to 50 per cent, and HEIs reporting figures between 3 per cent and 42 per cent. Most of the HEFCE-recognised funding consortia are operating with a figure below the mean for the system as a whole.

Indirect funding agreements differ in the information provided to colleges about the total resource provided by HEFCE for each student and how the proportions retained and passed on by HEIs are determined and justified. To understand and assess these calculations is not just a question of comprehending the HEFCE funding methodology and the range of responsibilities carried by the HEI. It is also a matter of fathoming the administrative, financial and quality systems (and assumptions and practices) operated internally by the HEI. Even where responsibilities and obligations on both sides are made explicit in a funding agreement, there is always the issue of how these are interpreted, reported and evaluated by each party.

Some of the most effective partnerships reflect the role of key individuals who manage the boundary between their course or their institution and the demands of a partner organisation. This is where the transaction costs of partnerships are so difficult to measure; and where collaborations without a strong infrastructure or strategic purpose are often more troubled than other (more secure) partnerships by the departure of a core member of staff. Partnerships can sometimes be over-dependent on the personal and professional commitments of 'boundary' people, especially if this work is not central to the strategic management and purpose of the institution.

For some colleges, there is a difficult decision to make about investing in the strengths and specialisms of a number of partner HEIs, or whether efficiency and other arguments favour a strategic alliance with one degree-awarding institution. Even if a single partnership is the chosen model, with perhaps some or all of the work of the college designated a university centre or organised in a higher education precinct, the day-to-day business of developing, approving and linking programmes will remain. The chapters that follow offer, we hope, some assistance to managers of partnerships in both sectors, especially where a variety of funding, curriculum and quality considerations bear on the conduct of collaboration.

Over and above their role in funding and quality assurance, partnerships between further and higher education institutions are at the centre of government efforts since 1997 to broaden the social base of undergraduate education, to meet regional needs for skills and to strengthen vocational and workplace progression. The first (and earliest) of these aims is associated with the establishment of widening participation partnerships in each of the English regions. The second is illustrated soon after by the creation of new technology institutes (NTIs) to expand the supply of people with technician and higher level skills in the area of information and communications technology.

The third (and latest) objective is manifest in Lifelong Learning Networks. Through collaboration on curriculum development, their main purpose is to extend local arrangements for students to move more easily between different kinds of vocational and academic programmes. Like the widening participation partnerships and NTIs before them, it is envisaged that LLNs will cover the whole country. Close to 100 colleges and 40 HEIs are in membership of the eight LLNs approved by the end of 2005.

Dimensions of difference

In this concluding section, we consider how different or distinctive the higher education delivered in further education is in comparison with that provided by institutions in the higher education sector. The question is important for two reasons. First, colleges in England are exhorted to focus their mission and, where possible, align their higher education with one or more of the vocational strengths in the further education curriculum. Similarly, differentiation is urged upon universities and other providers of higher education, to reflect contemporary demands for new combinations of skills and knowledge.

Second, there is an overlap in the English system between what colleges provide by way of higher education and what is offered in many universities and higher education establishments. As observed already, the overall share of higher education taken by the English colleges is modest, at least in comparison to systems such as that in Scotland. The character of this contribution is diverse, complex and changing. Nevertheless, it is the overlapping nature of this provision as much as its volume and variety that is part and parcel of the identity of higher education in the learning and skills sector.

That one in nine students undertake their higher education in further education is not an insignificant proportion. If the postgraduate population is excluded, then the college contribution is closer to one in eight. These proportions were sustained despite the slower expansion of undergraduate numbers in colleges than in HEIs and the attempt to relieve newly incorporated colleges of a provider role in higher education. Although colleges were never

uniform in their pattern of higher education, one of the conse-
quences of continuing with work at these levels was to extend the
range of qualifications and their modes of funding and delivery.

Today, colleges teach most of the students studying for HND and
HNC qualifications and about half those enrolled on Foundation
degrees, but institutions in the higher education sector still remain
the largest providers of undergraduate education at the certificate
and intermediate levels. In short, colleges and HEIs pursue a shared
mission in respect of higher education below the honours degree.
Proposals in the Dearing report to develop 'sub-degree' higher
education as a special mission for further education colleges soon
fell away and, when launched, there was no intention that the
Foundation degree should be delivered exclusively by these institutions. At least for the present, colleges are unable to lay claim to a
discrete level or part of higher education that is their own.

A major reason why the higher education sector is still so
heavily involved at the certificate and intermediate levels is its
near-monopoly of the DipHE and the Certificate of Higher
Education (CertHE). The separate development of this group of
qualifications reflected their early association with the colleges
of higher education and their later concentration in professional
subjects such as nursing and studies allied to medicine. Together,
the DipHE and CertHE account for over a third of enrolments at
these levels in the higher education sector. When the government
announced its intention to make the Foundation degree the
standard two-year qualification in English higher education, it
had the HND and HNC in its sights rather than the DipHE and
CertHE.

With no one type of undergraduate education specific to
further education, arguments for the distinctiveness of college-
based higher education rest mainly on its intimacy and pedagogy.
The crowded conditions of mass higher education are less a feature
of growth in further education. The smaller scales and personal
styles of teaching that continue within colleges, and which are
under pressure elsewhere, are key dimensions of difference. These,
it is claimed, sustain the high level of support for students and
their learning that is central to the purpose and ethos of further
education and which make this sector critical to widening participation in higher education. Through working in partnership with

local schools, employers and HEIs, colleges provide a responsive and supportive environment for the delivery of higher education:

They bring particular strengths in meeting local and regional skills needs and in improving local access for students in every community. They can offer experience and expertise in providing a supportive environment for learners, and have a track record in recruiting and mentoring non-traditional students. They need to continue to develop flexible modes of delivery and build routes for students to progress into higher education, whether at college or university.

(HEFCE 2005: 6–7)

Defending or challenging these claims is as much part of the management function as taking decisions on whether to continue or withdraw from higher education. Since higher education is always a minority provision in colleges, it must compete for attention and support from the rest of the college. Except where further and higher education is a joint mission, the dominant further education culture is likely to shape the character of the higher education effort. This might be to the advantage of higher education, anchoring it in the work of the college as a whole and building on expertise at other levels. Alternatively, it might serve to query or undermine the conduct of higher level programmes, underestimating the risks and opportunities involved and neglecting matters such as scholarly activity.

In future years, it is unlikely that the tasks associated with the management of higher education will become any less demanding, even if what colleges provide might become less differentiated or fragmented. On the contrary, it is reasonable to expect more volatility in the market for higher education, not just on account of variable fees but also with work-focused qualifications requiring renewal or replacement at shorter intervals. We return to these difficult questions in the final part of the book, where the strategic choices open to colleges with higher education are discussed. Before that, we devote separate chapters to each of the major aspects of higher education that require actions and decisions on the part of college managers.

3 Organisational arrangements and responsibilities

In Chapters 1 and 2, we looked at the shifting contexts for the development of higher education in further education and at changing patterns of provision. In this chapter, we focus on an institutional level and examine the forms of organisation which colleges have put in place in order to respond to funding, partnership arrangements and quality regimes; the following chapters examine each of these in more detail.

The provision of higher education in colleges is very variable in terms of mission, volume and funding route. Change and corresponding uncertainty generate a need for clarity of strategy and evaluation of the organisational arrangements, roles and responsibilities in colleges and their sustainability. Models of organisation are examined and a checklist of roles and responsibilities set out.

The issues will be of interest to:

- senior managers evaluating the fitness for purpose of a college's structures for managing higher education
- HE coordinators responsible for managing and coordinating aspects of higher education provision
- college HE programme leaders/curriculum managers
- quality, marketing and student support managers
- HEI link tutors or partnership managers.

Mission and purpose

Chapter 2 highlighted the diversity of patterns of higher education provision in colleges. Some colleges demonstrate strategically-driven growth; others, piecemeal and opportunistic evolution. Following the Foster Report and the White Paper *Further Education: Raising*

Skills, Improving Life Chances in 2006, the mission for the sector has been focused on the employability and progression of learners, and colleges are urged to evaluate their institutional mission. Where HE provision in colleges is of appropriate quality and is linked to their economic and social mission, it will be strengthened, in particular in regions where access to HE institutions is limited and through Lifelong Learning Networks (LLNs).

In 2005–06, close to 300 further education colleges were 'mixed economy institutions' funded to provide prescribed higher education courses. Of these 146 were directly funded, 30 were funded via one of the nine funding consortia and 265 were in receipt of funding for teaching students registered at HEIs with which the college had a collaborative arrangement (franchise). As these figures indicate, it is common for colleges to receive funding through more than one route (direct, franchise and consortium) and also to have more than one HEI partner (see Appendix A and Chapters 4 and 5). Of the colleges receiving direct funding (approximately half of the total), individual colleges had a total resource (HEFCE grant plus regulated fee income) ranging from close to £10 million to under £20,000. Student numbers ranged from well under 100 (into single figures) full-time equivalent numbers (FTEs) to over 2,000. Colleges, particularly the larger providers, may also have a significant proportion of non-HEFCE funded students (non-fundable, island and overseas).

There are a significant number of directly-funded colleges which are major providers of higher education (including those who are members of the self-identified 'mixed economy group' (MEG)) and a number of other colleges for whom their partnership with major franchisers is a prominent element of the college mission and HE strategy. However, for still other colleges, a small amount of provision (particularly HNDs, Fds and agreements for progression to top-ups) in a limited range of vocational areas is strategically appropriate.

Partnerships operate in a multitude of ways, from a course-by-course departmental relationship to a highly formalised multi-institutional partnership. They may also be regional subject-based collaborations (for instance for initial teacher training) or partnerships formed specifically for the development and delivery of Foundation degrees. Where a college has a range of partnerships, it is highly likely that each HEI and/or consortium will have different requirements and provide different forms and levels of support. The level of formality and the degree of detail of partnership arrangements continue to vary significantly, despite the publication in 1999 and 2000 of the HEFCE Codes of Practice for collaborative financial arrangements (see Chapter 5).

Since the 1992 Act, some, mainly specialist, colleges have joined the HE sector from the FE sector. Degree-awarding powers can be granted by the Privy Council (after advice from the Minister, in turn advised by the QAA); changes in 2004 to the criteria for award of university title have meant that an institution in the higher education sector can now be granted a university title without having to have the power to award their own research degrees. It may be that some colleges in the further education sector will wish to adjust their mission and delivery profile, but would need to meet the normal requirement of having at least 4,000 FTE higher education students of whom at least 3,000 are registered on degree-level courses (including Foundation degrees).

Organisation

The volume, nature and mix of funding streams and the concomitant relationships with HEFCE, with HEIs for indirect funding and/or with a consortium, require organisational responses which need to be reflected in administrative infrastructures and staffing. The other main issues to be addressed by colleges in their infrastructural arrangements are those of quality assurance, curriculum development, market analysis and marketing and the location and delivery of the higher education programmes.

Colleges demonstrate a wide range of arrangements for managing higher education provision, which may operate at a macro level with clearly defined structures and formally delineated roles and responsibilities, or may represent a more ad hoc response to specific external demands.

Representations of college organisation of higher education provision

Below we set out two 'ideal-type' characterisations of the range of organisational arrangements; each represents the intersection of two continua. In Figure 3.1, we set out the external drivers of HEFCE funding and partnership arrangements. In Figure 3.2, we demonstrate the internal arrangements for managing large and small provision either discretely or embedded, in parallel with further education provision, within the structure of the college.

Individual colleges are located throughout the four quadrants created by the continua Direct/Indirect funding and Contained/Permeating partnership in Figure 3.1, and Discrete/Embedded provision and Large/Small volume in Figure 3.2. In order to examine the diversity, we describe eight exemplars, one in each of the quadrants. These are placed in the figures at coordinates between the two axes, representing where they fall along the continua. They are identified as A, B, C, D and E, F, G, H.

A college needs to identify roles and responsibilities for the management of HE. This may be attached to a full or fractional post(s) or be allocated coordination time (remission), accompanied by appropriate committee structures. For each exemplar we identify the requirements that flow directly from the nature of partnership relationships (Figure 3.1), and the necessity for internal coordination across the college (Figure 3.2).

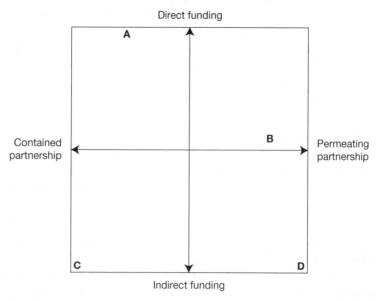

Figure 3.1 Funding and partnership

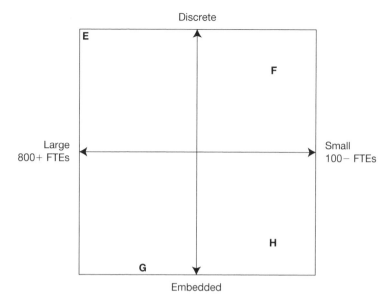

Figure 3.2 Organisation and size of college provision

These are, of course, ideal-type constructs and, while some colleges may correspond to one of these examples in all respects, the majority of managers will recognise a different position for their college.

The relationship between the four models in Figure 3.1 with those in Figure 3.2 is not direct and, in the following sections, we examine possible combinations.

Funding and partnership

Chapter 4 examines the principles and application of the HEFCE funding methodology and addresses the diversity and complexity of funding HE in FE colleges. That prescribed higher education which was funded by FEFC was transferred to HEFCE for 1999–2000, thus significantly increasing the number of HEFCE funded colleges. Colleges were asked to choose, from 2000–01 on, between continuing this direct funding, opting for indirect franchise funding or a new indirect option, that of membership of an 'HEFCE-recognised funding consortium', or a mixture (see Chapters 4 and 5). Generally speaking, partnerships for funding purposes are between an HEI and one or more colleges. However, the consortium arrangement can be led by a college and contain only further education members.

The vertical axis in Figure 3.1 reflects a continuum from provision fully directly funded to fully indirectly funded; for the purposes of this continuum, the two forms of collaborative arrangement, franchise and consortium, are equated. As noted earlier, the majority of colleges have two or three funding routes. The horizontal axis reflects the extent of partnership between a college and HEI(s) and other colleges. 'Contained' partnerships operate within defined boundaries; impacting on only a small number of roles within the institution. This may be a partnership with only one HEI (C) or, alternatively, partnerships which may be multiple but relate to only one or two aspects of provision and thus are restricted in their impact and demands on the college as a whole (A). 'Permeating' partnerships have an impact throughout the institutional structure and on roles and responsibilities at all levels. These partnerships may be defined by their range and multiplicity (and potentially competing demands on the college organizational structures) (B), or by high levels of commitment to and participation in a single formal arrangement between several partners (D).

The complexity of managing different funding streams and partnership relationships impacts on the cost to a college of funding its coordination, administration and management of higher education as a ratio to income. Where numbers are small but the provision is spread across the curriculum, the funding generated may not be sufficient to support dedicated management, but if HE-specific aspects of funding, data and quality are not managed in line with external requirements, the financial penalties incurred may further reduce the income. The degree of HE-specific management or coordination associated with the range of models of organisation reflects the need to liaise with external bodies (such as HEFCE and QAA) and with partner institutions. Even in colleges with a significant volume of HE provision, the difference between mainstream further and minority higher education activity can mean that the higher education programme leaders and curriculum managers are not integrated into the quality and management structure of the college and may experience isolation.

The following exemplars are provided to delineate possible organisational responses by colleges to issues of funding and partnership.

Exemplar A – fully directly funded with relationships with HEIs for validation purposes only

A college directly funded for all its prescribed higher education; it has no franchise partnerships with HEIs. This college provides HE programmes which are validated by two HEIs, one for the significant majority of the provision and another for a single course. The primary relationship is long-standing and the HEI has devolved much operational responsibility for quality assurance arrangements to the college – the college reports in to the HEI arrangements at the highest level. The programmes include those of the HEI, jointly written programmes and programmes written by the college for its particular client group. In addition, the college offers higher nationals under Edexcel's arrangements for HNs approved within the national qualifications framework (NQF); for this provision it has no quality assurance relationship with an HEI.

In this example, the college has a large volume of provision and the number of validation bodies (HEIs and Edexcel) and types of provision require designated management or coordination across the college and external liaison. While a provider of this type might manage HE as a discrete unit (as in exemplar E in Figure 3.2), a directly funded small provider with a single partnership might manage at programme level (exemplar F).

Exemplar B – significant amounts of direct funding and multiple partners for both franchise and validation

This college also has a large volume of provision. Much of it is directly funded and it has grown its provision through successful bids for additional student numbers (ASNs). However, it also has long-standing franchise partnerships and has forged new relationships recently in order to develop Foundation degrees within a dedicated partnership.

Given the size of the provision and complexity of funding, there is a need for substantial HE management or coordination to ensure consistency, oversee funding streams and manage relationships. Such a college may (as in exemplar E), or may not (G), manage its provision discretely.

Exemplar C – indirect funding via a single franchise partnership

This college has limited provision, only two courses in one subject area, and it is funded through a single partner HEI. The partnership is closely defined and the HEI manages data returns, admissions, curriculum and staff development and quality assurance, and retains a significant proportion or 'topslice' of the HEFCE funding. The partnership dimension, while formalised, is here characterised as 'contained' insofar as it is restricted to one partner.

The need for coordination and HE-specific managerial roles and responsibilities is minimal. The delivery and quality are addressed by the programme leader and the link tutor at programme level and liaison with the HEI over funding and related issues is the responsibility of a senior manager, with a remit for partnership work.

Exemplar D – indirect funding within an extensive partnership

This exemplifies a college with an explicit mission to provide substantial higher education which is funded primarily through either one of the 'major franchisers' or a large HEFCE-recognised funding consortium. An HEI may lead the multiple franchise collaboration or consortium or the college may lead a consortium itself. The relationship is well developed and embedded at the delivery and developmental level and at senior management and strategic levels. Clear documentation and memoranda of cooperation set out mutual roles and responsibilities and financial arrangements as proposed by the HEFCE codes of practice for sub-contractual relationships.

The partnership has an agreed regional vision and arrangements for developing, validating and delivering Foundation degrees.

Volume is large but, like B, this college might also be represented by E or G in Figure 3.2. Depending on whether management is discrete or embedded, the necessary liaison at all levels of the college managerial structure with the partner and in partnership decision-making structures will be allocated to designated managers or channelled through a cross-college coordinator and committee structures responsible for intra- and inter-institutional coordination.

Organisation of college HE provision

Decisions to embed or make discrete provision reflect the college mission and strategy. Differentiation by age, level and academic/vocational distinctions is variable across the sector's colleges. We have not addressed here the arrangements which might be generated by increases in the delivery of work-based higher education as encouraged in the HEFCE Strategic Plan for 2006–11 and the 2006 FE White Paper.

Figure 3.2 represents models of organisation within colleges. The vertical axis represents the degree to which provision is structurally discrete, possibly within an HE centre, or embedded within FE provision. The horizontal measures the volume of provision in full-time equivalent numbers (FTEs), with 'large' defined as over 800 and 'small' defined as under 100. These numbers (see Chapter 4) reflect HEFCE perceptions of minimum and significant critical mass. The degree of internal cross-college coordination required for each model is indicated.

The decision to embed HE provision within the college general provision or to provide it in a discrete unit is influenced by volume (exemplar E), but small provision may also be characterized as discrete insofar as it is sufficiently limited to be managed by a single experienced programme leader (F).

Where large provision is in a discrete centre (E), it supports the generation of an HE environment and HE experience for the students and clear management responsibilities for data management, strategic development and planning, quality assurance in line with

QAA requirements and curriculum development and continuous professional development. However, many large providers are committed to an embedded model (G) which they believe ensures subject expertise is applied to curriculum development and delivery and supports a commitment to a culture of a single college (for staff and students). This may also reflect a (common) perception of HE in FE as different and distinctive (as reported for instance in the LSDA research on higher education in the learning and skills sector, see Appendix C).

Where the volume of provision is medium or small, it is usually embedded, as there is unlikely to be sufficient volume of HE to warrant staff managing or teaching HE exclusively. This could result in a lack of a distinctive HE experience for students; it is expensive to provide continuous professional development for staff; and it can place undue burden on staff required to be familiar with both HE and FE. The dispersal of responsibility for delivery and monitoring can mean funding returns and projections are inaccurate, and the time necessary to coordinate in order to ensure meeting requirements of HEFCE and QAA may be disproportionate to income. However, for many small providers any such disadvantages are outweighed by the need to build on subject specialisms and to provide progression (H). In some cases, specialist dedicated arrangements may be appropriate to support regional subject-based collaboration (F).

Colleges couple their HE-specific quality assurance arrangements in a variety of ways and with varying degrees of formality and profile within the institution with their LSC-funded provision. Some colleges see no difficulty in reconciling their HE and FE systems, others believe a separate system is essential – this may be influenced by the volume of provision and funding streams, but not necessarily.

Some funding is available to support the enhancement of a higher education culture and delivery in colleges. Directly funded colleges with over 100 FTEs had access to the HE in FE development fund distributed from 1999 to 2000, and in the second phase (from 2002) colleges with over 800 FTEs were allocated double funding. This funding, which could be used to develop and reward staff and for capital (against an agreed strategy and action plan), was consolidated into teaching funding and earmarked capital from 2004–05 (see Chapter 4). For 2006–08 a Teaching Quality

Enhancement Fund will support quality enhancement and professional development (see Chapter 7). Colleges also received teaching and learning infrastructure for this period to help raise the quality of HE facilities, including e-learning resources, and to enhance the experience of their HE students. Again, this was allocated to colleges with over 100 FTEs (or aggregated in partnerships) and at twice the rate to those with over 800. Indirectly funded colleges can access both through their HEI funding partner(s) or consortium.

Exemplar E − high volume of provision in an HE centre

This represents a college with a large volume of provision which covers most subject areas and is a mix of vocational and academic and types of award (including the full range of: foundation years, Foundation degrees, 2+2 arrangements, higher nationals, bachelor and postgraduate degrees). The college has a clearly set-out HE strategy and has grown its provision by bidding for ASNs and through franchise relationships and Lifelong Learning Networks (LLNs).

This college has organised its HE provision into a physically and structurally discrete HE centre, with the dedicated senior managers reporting in to the college management, quality and governance structures at the highest levels. All the staff work solely on higher education provision, and curriculum and staff development are focused. As a directly-funded college with over 800 FTEs, it receives higher levels of developmental funding from HEFCE which supports discrete provision. The college manages non-prescribed higher education (NPHE) within the centre. Such arrangements simplify the application of HE-specific quality assurance arrangements and data monitoring and funding streams but, since there is more than one HEI partner and there is a direct relationship with Edexcel for higher nationals and with other awarding bodies for NPHE, quality assurance arrangements need to be differentiated.

A similar model may be funded via an extensive and formalized partnership arrangement which recognises and supports the HE curriculum offer and infrastructure of one or more colleges within the HEI's structural arrangements (see D in Figure 3.1).

Exemplar F – small provision managed within a specialist area

This provision is discrete insofar as it is limited to a sufficiently small number of courses that they can be managed by a single programme leader who is familiar with the HE-specific quality requirements. The provision may be directly funded, particularly if it is higher level provision within a specialist area (A), but it may have been developed with a local HEI and funded as a franchise (C).

As the provision is small, a cross-college role is unnecessary, but it is essential that the programme leader liaises closely with college managers with an understanding of the specificity of HE funding, data and quality processes.

Exemplar G – embedded substantial provision

This college has over 500 FTEs distributed across most subject areas but chooses to embed them within the schools of the college because managers consider that the client group for HE in FE is distinctive, and that the higher education programmes and client group have more in common with level 3 provision (including Access to HE courses), and because the vocational and work-related nature of much of the provision make it important to embed it within subject areas. Programme leaders may specialise in HE but in some of the schools there is only one higher level programme in a curriculum area and they and the teaching staff work on both FE and HE and prescribed and non-prescribed HE.

Because of the embedded and dispersed nature of the provision, cross-college coordination is essential at all levels from programme to strategic to ensure that the appropriate mechanisms are in place and funding returns and quality processes attended to.

Exemplar H – embedded small provision

Here a limited number of full and part-time programmes are embedded within the provision of a few schools. This may reflect the development of 'all-through' provision in vocational areas (perhaps in pursuit of CoVE status) or a 'second-chance' option to progress younger disadvantaged learners (linked to 14 to 19 flexibility initiatives) or for adult returners. Alternatively, it takes the form of modules of higher education provided to gifted and talented students and as a progression bridge to local HEIs.

The initiatives in the college are varied but they have in common the fact that they are higher education and thus need to be coordinated cross college rather than managed solely within the subject areas.

Where does a college sit in the matrices?

It may be useful for college managers to match their college to the exemplars and place it within the grids in order to evaluate their infrastructure for higher education provision and their strategic direction.

Considerations:

- What is the profile of higher education in the college? How does the volume and distribution across full-time and part-time numbers, level and subject reflect and/or determine strategic plans and organizational structures?
- Do senior managers monitor the HE provision and share the knowledge which will allow them to test the sustainability of the provision and manage uncertainty in a changing policy environment?

Roles and responsibilities

Whatever the volume and nature of the higher education provision in a college, there is a need for a clear locus of responsibility for both strategic and operational matters if provision of prescribed higher education is to be sustainable for a further education college. HE committees, developmental groups, programme approval arrangements and staff development programmes have a crucial role to play and the identified responsibilities of individual managers need to be well known. The HEFCE Supporting higher education in colleges: *Good practice guide* (see Appendix C) provides helpful guidance.

Where a college is working with one or more HEIs in a franchise relationship and/or other colleges within a consortium, it is important that the responsibilities within the college and within partner institutions are transparent, formally set out and consistently managed.

The range of tasks which need to be addressed within a college's management of higher education are summarised in Table 3.1 on pages 53–6. More detail is given in the following chapters.

Where is responsibility located?

Where provision is limited in volume and scope, programme leaders may have responsibility for the delivery of many or most of the tasks, but there will need to be mechanisms in place to ensure effective management of funding, data returns and quality. Where provision is more extensive, the day-to-day work of programme leaders may be managed directly or coordinated cross-college through identified roles and committee structures. Responsibility for planning and liaison with partners may be allocated to a manager or be the remit of a designated committee. In all cases, there need to be appropriate reporting mechanisms to committees and bodies such as Quality Committee, Academic Board and the Corporation.

Considerations:

- Where is responsibility located for each of the tasks? – centrally, with a cross-college role, with a particular department?
- is responsibility attached to named managers or to committees?
- are planning and liaison addressed?

Table 3.1 Checklists of tasks to be managed

Strategic	
Produce and monitor an HE strategy and action plan	Following the consolidation of the HE in FE development fund, there was in 2005–06 no requirement for directly-funded colleges to submit an HE strategy to HEFCE and the submission of widening participation strategies is no longer a condition of grant for HEIs following the requirement for access agreements submitted to the Office for Fair Access (Offa). Indirectly-funded colleges have never been required to set out a strategy and the extent to which they have been expected to feed into – or reflect – the strategy of funding HEI partners has been variable. However, a clear strategy for development, widening participation and regional partnership is essential in a changing policy environment in which college managers and governing bodies need to evaluate mission and performance. See Chapters 4 and 5.
Receive and evaluate guidance from HEFCE, QAA and Offa on funding and quality matters	Documentation will need to be disseminated to relevant staff. Indirectly-funded colleges will not normally receive documents directly but they are available via the relevant websites. See Chapters 4 and 6.
Monitor provision and make returns to HEFCE and to the LSC	It is essential that returns are timely and accurate. They may be made directly and/or by a partner HEI or consortium lead. Chapter 4 examines the funding methodology and the requirements for annual statistical returns.
Conduct market analysis	Strategic and curriculum development should be based on clear evidence of supply and demand. In the case of Foundation degrees, developments should be based on evidence of skills shortages and employer demand and willingness to cooperate in work-based learning as well as take into account the availability of feeder programmes and exits to honours degrees or other higher education.
Obtain additional funded places	Colleges seeking to grow their HE provision have had to obtain ASNs. These were introduced on a competitive basis in order to address identified priorities but for 2006–08 are embedded within regional strategic initiatives. See chapters 4 and 5.
Liaise with partners and participate in local/regional networks and initiatives	Partnerships range from informal to formal; from a single relationship at course level to an extensive partnership at institutional level. Roles and responsibilities need to be clearly set out in line with HEFCE and QAA codes of practice on collaborative arrangements. LLNs have been playing an increasing strategic role from 2005–06. See Chapter 5.

Table 3.1 Checklists of tasks to be managed (continued)

Engage with national networks and update specialist knowledge	HEFCE, QAA, the Association of Colleges (AOC), Foundation Degree Forward (FdF) the Learning and Skills Network (LSN) and the HE Academy all provide data sources, events and website support for HE in FE. See Appendix C.

Considerations:
- Does the college have a clear mission and strategy with regard to higher education and is this regularly monitored and updated?
- How does it relate to the college's overall mission and strategy and to regional priorities?
- Does the provision widen participation and enhance progression opportunities?
- How is the delivery and development of HE addressed in the planning and evaluation cycle of the college? Is it included in the self-assessment report (SAR)?
- Does the college management structure support the strategy for development and ensure compliance with HEFCE and QAA requirements (directly or via an HEI)?
- Is a risk analysis conducted to identify the potential impact of national and regional policies and initiatives?

Curriculum	
Curriculum development	Development of new programmes needs to take into account supply and demand as well as funding availability and necessary resourcing. The process of approval must address the QAA academic infrastructure, including its code of practice, framework for qualifications (FHEQ) and benchmark statements. Programme specifications for the course must be produced. Since 2001, some college/HEI partnerships have converted HNDs to Foundation degrees; conversions and new Fds must address the guidance from HEFCE and the QAA Foundation Degree Qualification Benchmarks (FDQB). Guidance from the Sector Skills Councils should also be taken into account. See Chapters 6 and 7.
Validation	HEIs operate varying validation arrangements (within QAA guidelines) for their awards, and those of Edexcel under licence. Edexcel provides NQF HNs within the QCA framework. A range of awarding bodies provide professional awards funded as NPHE but some of these qualifications, such as teacher training and management, are also validated and awarded by HEIs.
Ensure the quality of the HE experience for students	An appropriate environment needs to address the 'higherness' of the programmes and student experience. This is explored in Chapter 7.
Induction of staff into HE-specific systems	Whether at programme level, cross-college, or within an HE centre, staff development needs to address the particulars of the funding and quality assurance systems as well as subject or profession-specific updating. See Chapter 7.

Table 3.1 Checklists of tasks to be managed (continued)

Provide continuous professional development and support scholarly activity	The HE Academy leads on developing and supporting a standards framework for higher education. See Chapter 7.

Considerations:
- Does the development of programmes reflect a strategic direction and market analysis?
- Do programme development and validation arrangements ensure that external requirements are met?
- Is the learning experience provided to the higher education students appropriate to the level of their programmes, including staffing, resources and environment?

Quality assurance	
Produce consistent course and review documentation	Documentation needs to take account of QAA guidelines and the specific requirements of validating HEIs and/or Edexcel.
Meet external QA requirements	Where an HEI has validated a programme, quality assurance is the formal responsibility of the HEI: but mechanisms vary significantly. External examiners are appointed by and are responsible to the HEI. HNC/Ds may be delivered under the auspices of an HEI under licence or with direct responsibility to Edexcel and within the NQF of the QCA. Prescribed higher education falls within the responsibilities of the QAA. Non-prescribed higher level qualifications may also be delivered under the aegis of a range of awarding bodies accredited within the revised NQF at levels 4 to 8. See Chapter 6.
Operate internal quality assurance (QA) arrangements	The college needs to operate internal QA arrangements that will support preparation for awarding body scrutiny and Academic Review, where appropriate. Quality enhancement is a central element in the new QAA arrangements and colleges should ensure mechanisms are in place to utilise the feedback from external examiners and from students. See Chapter 6.
Participate in QAA review	Make preparation as a directly-funded institution covered by Academic Review and/or as part of the institutional audit or audit of collaborative provision of a partner. The QAA approach and proposed new method of review is described in Chapter 6 and compared and contrasted with that of Ofsted (and, previously, the Adult Learning Inspectorate (ALI)).

Considerations:
- Do arrangements for quality assurance of prescribed HE operate effectively in accordance with QAA guidelines and those of validating or franchising HEIs and/or of Edexcel?
- How do they articulate with the college QA arrangements for FE (and NPHE)?

Table 3.1 Checklists of tasks to be managed (continued)

Student support	
Market and recruit	Approaches to marketing are likely to reflect the internal arrangements for providing HE set out in Figure 3.2. HE-specific elements that must be addressed include the arrangements in place under the college's or partner HEI's access agreements, which must be published in a manner conveniently accessible to students and provide clear financial information covering the duration of a course. Fees policy will be influenced by any partnership arrangements the college has. See Chapter 4.
Oversee admissions	Managers need to ensure that college provision is listed in UCAS and organise HE-specific admission arrangements with designated staff, including during Clearing. Application and enrolment forms must capture the data required for the statistical returns. See Chapter 4.
Provide student information, guidance and support	Managers need to ensure that the eligibility criteria for HE funding are clear and that students are advised about Disabled Students Allowance (DSA) support. Applicants must be made aware of their rights with regard to student loans, grants, bursaries and fee waivers. See Chapter 4.
Considerations: • Does the college market HE separately? If not, are the specific elements relating to eligibility, fees and financial support addressed? • Where a college is in a partnership, are the marketing materials agreed? • Does student support within the college address HE-specific requirements?	

4 Funding: principles and practice

In this chapter, we address the funding of higher education in further education colleges. We examine the complexity and variety which flow from the scope and operation of the two funding councils - HEFCE and FEFC/LSC – and from the change from 1999 in responsibilities for funding prescribed higher education delivered in colleges. As described in Chapter 1, this resulted in over 200 colleges being funded by HEFCE, in addition to the 72 funded at that time.

The issues will be of interest to:

- senior managers using an overview of the funding of HE in FE to inform strategic decisions about college income streams and partnerships and for planning organisational infrastructures
- finance managers accounting for income from HE provision
- information systems managers responsible for data returns to HEFCE or to funding partners
- curriculum managers and HE coordinators responsible for delivery of HE programmes and for supplying monitoring data
- managers with oversight of the admissions process
- student support managers overseeing the information and guidance provided to higher education students
- marketing managers describing the college's HE product.

The volume and nature of provision of higher education in further education colleges is very variable, as is its historical development. While some colleges have very small provision, others have extensive provision; HEFCE funding policy documents have reflected this in the Council's consideration of direct and indirect funding. There is no direct relationship between volume and direct funding, however – while the 'major providers' (defined by having over 500 full-time equivalent numbers – FTEs) are primarily directly funded, a significant proportion have no or few directly-funded FTEs but are funded via consortia and/or franchise partners. For 2005–06,146 colleges were directly funded, with total resource (grant plus assumed regulated fee income) ranging from close to £10 million to under £20,000. Twenty-three colleges received a grant of over £2 million and 25 of over £1 million, but 58 received less than £500,000, with a significant proportion in receipt of under £100,000.

Funding of higher education provided in further education colleges

Funding principles

In 2003, HEFCE consulted on its teaching funding method; it incorporated some minor changes and embarked on a major review. Formal consultation was initiated on the proposals flowing from the review in 2005, taking a two-cycle approach with the first cycle expected to last until the outcome of the proposed government review of fee income in 2009. In 2005–06, and for 2006–07, the method is essentially unchanged but with a funding uplift, in order to retain stability in funding as the sector prepared for the introduction of the new variable fee regime and the dynamic environment created by the 2004 Higher Education Act.

The original HEFCE model (implemented in 1993–94) reflected the fact that the funding bodies which preceded HEFCE funded different institutions at different rates for different reasons. After fundamental review in 1995, a new method was implemented from 1998–99 for the 134 HEIs then funded, and from 1999–2000 for the 286 colleges directly funded in that year (including over 200 transferring from FEFC funding). This methodology was subsequently subject to only minor modification and was underpinned by two broad premises:

- that similar activities should be funded at similar rates
- that institutions wanting additional student numbers should bid for them.

Proposed changes which may be implemented from 2007–08 are addressed later in this chapter.

After the decision to transfer any FEFC-funded prescribed higher education to HEFCE for 1999–2000, colleges were asked to choose for 2000–01 between continuing direct funding of this provision or transferring it to an indirect franchise relationship with an HEI or through a new arrangement of a funding consortium (see Appendix B for a chronology of funding initiatives). In each subsequent year, colleges could apply to change funding routes. For the purposes of funding, these two types of collaborative arrangements are defined in HEFCE documentation (see below), but the terms 'franchise' and 'consortium' have common alternative uses with regard to partnership and curriculum (see Appendix A and Chapters 5 and 7):

Franchise: applies to virtually all collaborative funding arrangements, including many that colleges may refer to as consortia, such as for the delivery of Foundation degrees. Where a student is registered at one institution but taught at another this is described as a franchise. The funding flows from HEFCE to the franchising institution and the proportion passed on is subject to the particular arrangement between the partner institutions.

Consortium: this term only applies to 'HEFCE-recognised funding consortia'; it is a mechanism for distributing grant to a group of institutions through a single lead institution. In 2005–06 there were nine consortia, three of which were led by colleges. Here the funding from HEFCE passes to the lead institution but the students are registered at the partner delivering the programme. This has implications both for statistical returns (see below) and for the responsibility for quality (see Chapter 6).

The number of directly-funded colleges has fallen year-on-year since 1999–2000. While it is recognised that there is a case for particular types of small provision to be directly funded, the funding council has consistently drawn attention to the likely benefits for quality and the learner experience in establishing collaborative arrangements with HEIs, and some smaller providers have chosen to be funded indirectly. However, the majority of the changes from direct to indirect funding were in the first three years and most of these were the result of the formation of strategic multiple partnerships, both franchise and consortium, including, in 2002–03 and 2003–04, the three FE-led consortia. In other cases, larger providers have merged with or set up collaborative HE centres with universities and, in some cases, colleges have transferred to the HE sector.

Further education colleges providing higher education directly funded by HEFCE have been subject to the same teaching funding methodology as higher education institutions from 1999–2000, but certain elements do not apply. There is no access to research funds and restricted access to capital funding and special initiatives (such as the Higher Education Innovation Fund (HEIF)), reflecting the primary responsibility of the LSC for the institutional infrastructure. However, increasingly, developmental funding, including capital funding for the teaching and learning infrastructure has been made available to directly-funded colleges, and to indirectly funded colleges through HEIs and to indirectly-funded colleges through HEIs or consortia (see Table 4.1 pages 62–4). The FE White Paper flagged up requests to HEFCE and the LSC to explore mechanisms for providing capital support, including direct funding of HE facilities in colleges and review of the financial arrangements that underpin HE courses in FE, including franchising arrangements.

The LSC has powers to fund non-prescribed higher education.

Application of the HEFCE teaching funding methodology
Directly-funded colleges are included with HEIs in the allocation and monitoring of funding, but benchmarks of 100 FTEs and 800 FTEs are applied to certain funding streams. Indirectly-funded colleges are subject to the application of the methodology to their partner HEI and their student numbers are part of the HEI's calculation. The amount of funding passed on is variable and while that funding passed on may reflect a detailed breakdown of what each partner is providing, this is not always the case (see Chapter 5), and thus colleges may engage in similar activities at differential rates of funding.

The funding methodology as operated in 2005–06 is outlined in Table 4.1 pages 62–5. Allocations are made following an annual cycle with provisional allocations in February and grant adjust-ments in July (the timeline and action required is outlined in Table 4.2). All aspects of the cycle and the application of the method-ology are clearly set out in HEFCE documentation including, annually, *Funding higher education in England. How HEFCE allocates its funds*. Colleges with no direct funding do not routinely receive documentation from HEFCE but can access the website for infor-mation (see Table 4.2 and Appendix C).

While based on formulae, the grant is a block grant and the funding agreement drawn up each year allows institutions to vary their recruitment so long as the volume of activity of FTE students across price groups is maintained within the 5 per cent tolerance band. For colleges with small provision, the ability to vary recruitment is likely to be restricted. Where funding is indirect (franchise or consortium) the college needs to work collaboratively with partners to monitor and adjust numbers. Colleges which have low retention rates are particularly vulnerable to funding adjust-ments. Colleges with indirect funding arrangements may also find that under-recruiting HEI partners wish to adjust the allocation of student numbers to the college.

The detail of the application of the formulae and its dependence on the accuracy of data provided by the universities and colleges has significant financial implications for colleges if their data management does not meet HEFCE requirements: this is examined in the section on data management pages 69–73.

Funding developments

The review of the teaching funding method is taking a two-cycle approach. The first cycle, from 2005–06, is addressing issues that require attention and is expected to last at least until the outcome of the government's planned review of fee income in 2009. The earliest any elements could be introduced would be for 2007–08.

The broad principle of similar resources for similar activities is contested within higher education, with institutions arguing, from different perspectives, that their provision is more cost-intensive (i.e. dissimilar) and, thus, for favourable weighting of either provision or of types of student.

It is recognised that fee deregulation is likely to increase diversity in higher education. HEFCE is proposing to put in place a method

Table 4.1 Summary of funding and key implications for further education colleges
All examples and references relate to funding for 2005–06

Funding stream	Element of funding	Calculation of grant	Application to colleges
Teaching	Main element	*Standard resource* calculated based on: • number of students (home undergraduate FTEs, previous year's numbers plus allocated ASNs) • subject-related factors (4 price groups A–D, numbers weighted 4, 1.7, 1.3, 1) • student-related factors (long courses, part-time students, Fd students) • institution-related factors (London weighting, specialist institutions, small institutions, old and historic buildings). This is a notional calculation of what the institution would get if its grant was calculated afresh each year. *Assumed resource* calculated based on teaching grant actually paid previous year, adjusted (for: previous year's recruitment and retention, inflation, ASNs, any mainstreamed grants), plus assumed fees. Where a difference is within the tolerance band of 5 per cent, grant is carried forward. Where outside (+/−) 5 per cent, grant and/or student numbers are adjusted.	Only 3 price groups (not A – clinical studies) Only London weighting is available to FECs The base price (including assumed fee, see below) for 2005–06 was £3,608 for band D, £4,690 for C and £6,134 for B. LSC rates (including assumed fee) for listed (NQF) courses and loadbanded (Other, including Access to HE and NPHE), determined by guided learning hours (GLH), are set out in the LSC *Funding Guidance* and weighted from 1.0 (A) to 1.72 (E). For directly-funded colleges, data is taken from the Higher Education in Further Education Students (HEIFES) survey and retention data from the Individualised Learner Record (ILR) (the July FO4) is used to reconcile. For indirectly-funded colleges, data is from the HEI's Higher Education Students Early Statistics (HESES) survey reconciled with the HEI's Higher Education Statistics Agency (HESA) return (see the section on data management). Note, only students who 'complete' (either by undergoing the final assessment for or passing the programme are eligible for funding (unlike the LSC three-period on-programme plus achievement formula): however, partial completion is being addressed under the proposals for a

Widening participation	*Widening access*: Full-time and part-time undergraduates weighting for educational disadvantage based on data from HESA or LSC showing census ward and weighted by participation rate or average educational attainment in the ward. *Improving retention*: allocated on basis of pre-entry qualifications and age for full-time undergraduates; pro rata to London-weighted FTEs for part-time undergraduates. *Disabled students*: allocated on proportion of students in receipt of DSA.	It is essential that relevant student records contain accurate data – FE staff may not be alert to the categories used for funding allocations. HEFCE has warned colleges that previous ILR data used for this purpose was poor.
Rewarding and developing staff in HE (R&DS)	Previously specific funding was made available to reward and develop staff but these allocations were consolidated into the teaching grant in 2004–05. There is funding for recruitment and retention (dance and drama, golden hellos and promising researchers). These strands and Round 2 R&DS are separately identified and subject to separate monitoring.	Colleges were not able to access the specific funds but funds for R&DS incorporated into the HE in FE Development Fund (from 2000) were available to directly funded FECs (with over 100 FTEs) and consolidated in 2004–05. Recruitment and retention strands are not available.
Research	General funds to support the research infrastructure.	Colleges not eligible.
Special funding	Range of funds each year for specific initiatives (which may then be phased out or consolidated).	Not available (unless in partnership with an HEI).
Earmarked capital funding	Previously for particular initiatives, most recently science research, learning and teaching and IT. For 2006–08 a single fund was announced to support the infrastructure for learning, teaching and research. Funding distributed by formula as a conditional allocation, with HEIs required to submit proposals for spending. Allocations to HEIs include a specified amount related to their franchised student numbers. The lead institution of a consortium receives funding for all members.	Directly-funded colleges received some capital funding through the HE in FE Development Fund. For 2005–06 colleges were allocated capital funding to raise the quality of teaching and learning resources on the same basis as the Development Fund (i.e. only to colleges with over 100 FTEs and double rate to those with over 800. Colleges with less than 100 could access the funds in collaboration with other colleges or HEIs). For 2006–08 this will be used to parallel the support to HEIs for the teaching and learning infrastructure. Indirectly-funded colleges must access through their lead HEI. The 2006 FE White Paper proposed capital support.

Table 4.1 Summary of funding and key implications for further education colleges (continued)
All examples and references relate to funding for 2005–06

Additional Student Numbers (ASNs)	Annual competitive bidding against criteria was introduced for ASNs in 1998–99. The criteria prioritised growth in access and sub-degree work. For the 2003 bidding round only Foundation degrees were available. The new method introduced for 2006–08 focused on strategic regional growth. ASN targets must be met (overall FTEs) or funding is withheld, with a chance in the second year to recruit and retain the numbers.	Directly-funded colleges with over 100 FTEs can apply. Smaller providers are encouraged to collaborate and indirectly-funded colleges were referred to Circular 99/36. Fds must be validated by an HEI and active partnership be demonstrated.
Fees	Assumed fee income is taken into account in the calculation of total HEFCE resource. In 2005–06 this was the regulated fee or sector average: £1,175 for full-time and £1,140 per FTE for part-time undergraduates. The fee historically represented about one quarter of the income associated with the costs of teaching a full-time undergraduate but fees became variable (up to £3,000) from 2006–07. For 2006–07, the total resource will continue to be calculated using the regulated fee income at the 'basic amount' permitted under the 2004 Act, rather than the 'higher amount'.	The LSC assumed fee increased for adults from 25 per cent to 27.5 per cent for 2005–06 with planned increases to 37.5 per cent by 2007–08. The 2006 FE White Paper proposes a 50 per cent contribution by 2010. For franchise students it is assumed that the HEI will collect the fee. If the college collects it and it is offset against the HEFCE grant passed on, it is deemed to have been transferred. If colleges charge less than the assumed fee for part-time students, they create a position where they are, in effect, under-resourced against the assumed total resource.

	Access Agreements must be in place for institutions planning to charge more than £1,200 from 2006–07 and reviewed annually.	HEI partners may require colleges to set the same fee (to the maximum of £3,000) and different partners may set different fees (see section on learner support). The unit of resource for 2006–07 has been calculated on the basis of inclusion of the 'basic amount' of permitted fee, but where colleges do not charge above this they will be relatively disadvantaged.
Medical and dental education and teacher training	Funding for medical and dental education and research is distributed through a partnership between HEFCE and the National Health Service (NHS). The Training and Development Agency for schools (TDA) provides funding for education and training courses aimed at school teachers.	No price band A students or funding. Teacher training provided by colleges is generally for the FE sector. It may be validated by an HEI or non-prescribed; in the former case it will receive HEFCE funding, in the latter, LSC.

for funding teaching that will support and protect its strategic priorities. The new method will, in most respects, maintain the same basic structure but will introduce targeted allocations to address strategic aims. In the current method, premiums recognise additional costs, as does the widening participation allocation which has been, and continues to be, increased since its introduction in 1999–2000.

Elements of the proposals have particular significance for colleges which tend to have missions to widen participation and higher numbers of non-traditional students and part-timers, and lower completion rates. This includes the proposal to adjust the premium funding, to make a fee assumption of £2,000 and to explore funding of partial completion as measured by credit awarded.

The outcomes of the first cycle of consultation were reported in March 2006. The principle of providing similar resources for similar activities is retained and underpins the decisions. No changes to price groups are proposed in the short term but a full economic costing of teaching activity will be carried out using a Transparent Approach to Costing (TRAC), which will inform future consideration of the funding method. TRAC is not, however, used in colleges and HEFCE will work with a group of college finance directors to address the issue of costing HE in colleges. Consultation on proposals for a national framework for costing teaching is planned for autumn 2006.

The fee assumption for 2006–07 (£1,200) only reflects an inflationary increase, but it was proposed to increase the assumed fee to £1,750 for 2007–08 and to £2,000 in 2008–09. The figure of £2,000 was based on an assumption of bursaries or equivalent benefits averaging £1,000 for each full-time undergraduate. However, in the light of the (varied) responses from HEIs and colleges, it was decided to explore the issue further, with a final decision by December 2006.

In 2005–06, funding associated with premiums operated within the tolerance band (i.e. an institution would only attract extra funding if the premium resulted in it moving below the 5 per cent tolerance band). Under the proposal to replace premiums with a system of allocations operating outside the tolerance band this would be 'real' money not attached to the main formula (but within the block grant). This will be pursued but not operated until 2008–09 at the earliest.

Critical mass and partnership

HEFCE is not a planning body (as the FEFC was not) and thus does not prescribe actions. However, it does have strategic objectives and priorities in which it can invest. The funding council has consistently expressed concerns regarding the potential risk to the quality of the student experience where small pockets of HE are taught in isolation, and has encouraged collaborative partnership between colleges and HEIs (through indirect funding) and between colleges, including directly-funded colleges with fewer than 100 FTEs. As noted in Chapter 1, the 2006 FE White Paper, while supporting the role of colleges in delivering HE, asserted that where colleges are not delivering to the right standard, HE provision should not continue, and asked HEFCE to review the effectiveness of small pockets of HE in colleges.

In 2000, after colleges had been asked to choose between funding options, HEFCE reported that of the 283 further education colleges, 70 opted for direct funding only; 81 indirect only (46 franchise, 25 consortium, 10 franchise plus consortium); 132 indirect and direct (110 franchise plus direct, 8 consortia plus direct and 14 franchise plus consortium plus direct).

By 2004–05, of the 290 colleges providing higher education, 24 were in receipt of direct funding only; 138 indirect only (112 franchise, 7 consortium, 19 franchise plus consortium); 128 indirect and direct (121 franchise plus direct, 7 franchise plus consortium plus direct).

Any changes to funding routes or transfers of funding and numbers must be agreed by mid-April for grant for the next academic year.

The HE in FE Development Fund announced in 2000 was restricted to colleges with over 100 FTEs (or collaborating colleges with an aggregate of over 100) so that the fund could be used to encourage a critical mass sufficient to sustain the quality, standards and culture properly associated with the experience of higher education. In the second phase of this funding (introduced in

2002), colleges with over 800 FTEs were provided with twice the rate of funding compared to those with 100 to 799, in order to help the largest providers to build their critical mass and strengthen quality and range of provision: and this approach continues in the allocations for capital funding. Similarly, invitations to bid for ASNs, while reflecting the drive to expand access, particularly in Fds and through further education colleges, have consistently encouraged small providers to collaborate rather than to make individual bids.

The 2005 round of bidding for ASNs for 2006–07 and 2007–08 was tied in part to the Strategic Development Fund (SDF) set up following the 2003 White Paper. The new method made numbers available for 'strategic' and 'managed' growth. The former related to strategic projects already agreed or in an advanced stage of preparation, including Lifelong Learning Networks, and was only allocated to HEIs within the higher education sector and thus only accessible to colleges working in partnership with an HEI leading an SDF project. The latter was growth meeting national or regional demands where the proposals were brokered by the HEFCE regional consultants. In reviewing proposals for managed growth for 2006-08, HEFCE expected 50 per cent of the numbers to go to Foundation degrees and took into account the size of HE provision in colleges, not expecting to receive proposals from colleges with fewer than 100 directly funded FTEs. Provisional allocations for 2006–07 included £38 million for strategic and managed growth and an additional £6 million awarded to LLNs and channelled through eight lead HEIs (outside their mainstream teaching grant).

The 2006 FE White Paper supported an important and growing role for FE colleges in providing higher education within a focus on employability. The presumption should be that the provision will be occupationally orientated and that the major area of expansion should be Foundation degrees and work-based HE programmes. HEFCE was charged to treat these and provision within 'centres of HE excellence' in colleges with a mission to support employability and to widen participation as a priority.

Data management

The HEFCE grant for teaching is calculated on the basis of early statistical returns (the Higher Education Students Early Statistics

Considerations:

- Is the HE provision greater or less than 100 FTEs and how does this impact on the college's HE strategy?
- What is the income generation of the HE provision (including international students) and is cross-subsidy occurring (FE to HE or HE to FE)?
- To what extent do national and/or regional and local imperatives drive or override financial considerations?
- If the college is in receipt of franchise and/or consortium funding, are the terms of the financial agreement clear and are all premium weightings and additional funding streams transferred?
- Is there an infrastructure in place within the college to support data management and strategic planning of HE in line with the requirements of HEFCE or a franchising HEI and/or a consortium, as appropriate?
- If appropriate, who is the lead on liaison with franchising HEIs and/or consortia? Who will participate in regional networks and LLNs?

(HESES) survey or the Higher Education in Further Education: Students (HEIFES) survey) recording the number of FTE students attending (or forecast to attend) in the year, and estimated completions. These are then reconciled after the end of the academic year with HESA or LSC individualised student data records. Where significant discrepancies are established, this impacts on the funding allocation and can lead to 'holdback' of funding from future grant. HESA and LSC individualised student data is also used to calculate the widening participation allocations for the future grant (i.e. 2004–05 data for 2006–07 grant).

Where a college is funded through a franchise relationship, the partner HEI(s) is required to make the returns for all the franchised students and record the students on HESA. The lead institution in a recognised funding consortium is required to make the early return for all the student numbers funded via the consortium. However, for funding consortia students are recognised as students of the individual consortium member, and they should be reported on the HESA or the LSC individualised returns of the consortium members.

Below we set out the timeline for managing the funding relationship with HEFCE. Where a college is directly funded, HEFCE will liaise directly; where a college is indirectly funded via one or more franchise or consortium relationships, the student numbers will be included in the allocations to the HEI or consortium lead and no direct communication will generally take place with HEFCE (though HEFCE may contact consortium members directly as part of the HESA/HESES or ILR/HEIFES reconciliation exercise). Any errors in the data are the responsibility of the institution and, if identified during audit or the reconciliation of the early statistic returns and the individualised learner records, will lead to adjustment of funding and/or student numbers.

For colleges, the complexity of managing the different funding systems is compounded by the fact that the majority have more than one source of HE funding and may have multiple partnership relationships, including both franchise and consortium. The Foster Review in 2005 recognised this burden of bureaucracy and recommended consideration of a single-purpose agency for collection and synthesis of data covering both FE and HE: the DfES accords this a high priority and in the White Paper noted it was exploring options, including giving HESA new responsibilities for post-16 data.

The reconciliation process between the early returns and the individualised student records is a detailed, and extended process

Table 4.2 The annual funding cycle illustrated with references to HEFCE documentation in the 2005–06 academic year

---

February
Individual institutions receive a letter from HEFCE setting out their provisional allocation of recurrent grant for the next academic year (28 February 2005); grant tables are attached. Copies are on the HEFCE extranet, which is accessed using allocated 'keys'.

   No action is required unless institutions wish to implement any changes in their funding relationships (i.e. shifts between direct and indirect funding or formation of new consortia).

March
Provisional distribution of all grants is announced in a circular (2005/13).

Table 4.2 The annual funding cycle illustrated with references to HEFCE documentation in the 2005–06 academic year (continued)

May
Deadline for institutions to request amendments to provisional allocations, including amendments to the previous ILR data, which is used to calculate the widening participation allocations.

July
After any corrections to data have been made, the final grant is allocated in late July. A Funding Agreement is issued to each institution with student number targets and contract range.

Arrangements for application of subsequent grant adjustments (i.e. as a consequence of over or under recruiting against contract – normally the 5 per cent tolerance band – are published (2005/33).

September
HEIFES and HESES documentation issued.

September/October
The end-of-year individualised student records (HESA or LSC FO4) are returned. Later in the year, HEFCE uses these to reconcile with the early statistical returns and confirm the previous year's outturn against the allocation (there is a year's timelag). HESA and ILR data are also used to calculate the widening participation funding for the next year.

November/December
The annual survey is completed by HEIs and directly-funded colleges and by funding consortia's lead institutions.

HEIs complete HESES05 for 1 December census and colleges complete HEIFES05 for 1 November census.

Survey tables are available on the extranet in November. Returns are uploaded. Return dates are specified (22 November for colleges, 8 December for HEIs) and requests for late submission are not accepted.

HEFCE runs validation and credibility checks and writes to institutions asking them to verify the data and submit any appeals for mitigation of consequential grant adjustments.

January
All institutions must have authorised and signed off (at a senior level) the early statistics data.

February
Institutions are notified of final grant adjustments (i.e. to the current academic year's grant), including the outcome of appeals.

All standard documentation and workbook templates are available on the HEFCE website and can be accessed for information by colleges not in receipt of direct funding who will not otherwise receive them. www.hefce.ac.uk includes guides to HEFISES and HESES, exemplar grant letters and explanatory guidance.

and final confirmation of the out-turn position may impact on more than one year's funding allocations. Where a college demonstrates a significant difference between their HEIFES return and the HEIFES re-creation based on the ILR above a threshold, they may be selected for a monitoring exercise and required to produce an action plan. For franchising colleges the time lag in funding adjustments may be further increased.

Noting that funding adjustments may be significant, HEFCE stresses the importance of colleges ensuring that sufficient time and resources are allocated to allow the exercise to be completed accurately and promptly. Audits carried out during 2005 revealed a continuation of a significant number of common errors in HEIFES returns, including a lack of knowledge management. This suggests that many directly-funded colleges are not sufficiently familiar with their data requirements and that inadequacies in data collection and monitoring have led both to under-funding (in relation to the widening participation elements) and to holdback where under-recruitment occurred or retention is lower than projected.

Indirectly-funded colleges need to be aware of the detail of the funding and monitoring process and ensure that their partner HEI has accurate data for the HESA record. The audit of HEI's HESES data in 2005 found evidence of poor communication within collaborative arrangements and HEFCE stressed that it is essential that exchanges of information between all partners are frequent, timely, open and effective, and suggested that when entering into partnership arrangements, the systems in operation and exchange of information should form part of the negotiations and final agreement (see Chapter 5). It is recommended that partner colleges use the lead institution's standard forms.

A web facility was set up in 2004 and colleges are expected to look there for guidance on making HEIFES returns and encouraged to use it as part of their data-quality processes before making their returns to the LSC in September. A review of the use of the web facility revealed that colleges not using it were more likely to have been selected for the monitoring exercise.

HEFCE organise regular workshops for MIS managers.

It is proposed in the longer term to cease using HESES and HEIFES data for funding purposes, with the new teaching funding method relying on HESA and the ILR: this was the subject of consultation in 2005 on the review of the funding method. Implementation of this proposal would at the earliest use end-of-year data for 2008–09.

Considerations:

- Are the mechanisms in place and responsibilities clearly located to ensure timely and accurate returns to HEFCE, directly or via a partner HEI?
- Are relevant managers familiar with the HEFCE documentation and guidance and accessing the web facility?
- Where applicable, are at least two people able to manage the HEIFES return?
- Are HESA or ILR data returns accurate in order to support the full funding claim?
- Are retention projections (estimated completions) against census (for HEIFES or HESES) accurate?
- Are projected funding for HE provision and possible adjustments to funding in subsequent years addressed in business plans and accounts?
- Does the process of admission and tuition fee collection reflect the requirements of HEFCE and are all necessary data fields collected?

Support for learners

Eligibility of learners

LSC and HEFCE define a home student differently for the purposes of funding; as a consequence, there were categories of learner who had been eligible for funding for HE programmes from the FEFC who were no longer eligible when funding transferred to HEFCE in 1999–2000, that is, those refugees and asylum seekers who did not meet the fees and awards regulations definition. In addition, these learners may be ineligible to progress (unless as an 'overseas' student) from a level 3 programme (such as

Access) in FE to an HE programme, whether at a college or an HEI. When that HE programme is provided in the same college, the rationale is unlikely to be clear to the student concerned and the implications of the regulations were not immediately obvious to many colleges in 1999.

Definition of a home student

For HEFCE, 'home' students are defined as those who are eligible for home fees under the Education (Fees and Awards) Regulations (as amended in 1997 and effective from 1 September 1997). Home students are defined by the admitting institution interpreting the regulations: that is, settled in the UK (within the meaning of the Immigration Act 1971); 'ordinarily resident' in the UK; or, in the case of EU students the European Economic Area, for three years preceding the course, provided that no part of that three year period was wholly or mainly for the purpose of receiving full-time education.

The Regulations apply to both the higher education and the further education sector as defined in the F & HE Act 1992, however, the FEFC decided to include additional groups as eligible for funding as a home student, including those persons who had been in the UK legally for 3 years without the requirement to be settled or with any conditions attached to the purpose of residence. Further, the FEFC/LSC defined persons eligible for funding as those groups corresponding to the Regulations, i.e. 'home students' (including EU and EEA migrant workers), but added asylum seekers in receipt of state assistance and those with recently settled status.

Financial support

The funding councils' different approaches to fee waiver and to part-time fees had a negative impact on funding for college programmes at the point of transfer, which was partly addressed by adjusting the support funds (then Access Funds) available in higher education (with an extension to cover fee remission for eligible part-time students). Funds for directly funded HE in FE were channelled via the FEFC, and for franchise accessed via the HEI. Access Funds were subsequently reconfigured into a range of support funds and bursaries for personal support. Learner support managers need to be familiar with the current funding streams and HE student eligibility and alert to whether application procedures are channelled via funding partners.

Information on student financial support can be accessed via the DfES portal or directly on www.direct.gov.uk.

In January 2006, the DfES published *Improving the Student Finance Service. Report of the Review of Higher Education Student Finance Delivery in England* and in July 2006, the Minister announced the implementation of the recommendations. The Student Loans Company (SLC) will be reformed and become the customer-focused national delivery organisation to be available for students applying in Sepember 2008 for 2009–10 entry. This will involve an integrated online service, including a financial calculator for students giving information about their entitlement to statutory support and to compare bursary offers from different institutions (see access agreementss below).

For 2006–07, changes to fee grant and support for part-time students from the Access to Learning Fund (ALF) were introduced, but this will not address fully the likely impact of variable fees for full-timers on pro rata fees for part-timers and the fact that part-timers must pay fees 'up front'. Further, students are defined and funded as 'part-time' in the expectation that they are studying 50 per cent or more of a full-time programme, whereas part-time students may wish to study a smaller proportion. The HE Academy will develop a long-term strategy to respond to work-based learning.

Under the LSC Additional Learning Support model, a college responds to individual student claims for a range of support on programme. However, HEFCE-funded students are required to make an application to their local authority for the Disabled Students Allowance (DSA) which is paid to assist students who can show they have a disability or medical condition that affects their ability to study. It is incumbent on HEIs and colleges to ensure that applicants are aware of their responsibilities to make these arrangements before they start the course. Tutors in colleges commonly have a responsibility to refer FE students in need of support to a central student support system for diagnostic assessment or directly to drop-in learning centres, but HE students are not eligible for support systems funded by the LSC and this can create difficulties if staff are unaware of the funding differences and a dedicated HE system is not in place. For colleges delivering HE under franchise arrangements, the responsibility and channels for providing support can be blurred.

Fees and access agreements

The Higher Education Act of 2004 established the principle of variable fees and established a Director of Fair Access to ensure, through the approval of access agreements, that the introduction of variable (up to £3,000) tuition fees in 2006–07 did not have a detrimental effect on widening participation. All institutions directly funded by HEFCE deciding to raise their full-time under-graduate fees above the standard (£1,200) were required to submit an access agreement for 2006–07 to the Office for Fair Access (Offa) for approval by March 2005. Institutions are expected to invest a proportion of the additional tuition fee income (i.e. that over and above the standard fee) in bursary and/or other financial support for students and/or in outreach work in order to attract increased numbers of applications from under-represented students, in particular students from low income groups. If funding is via an HEI, then it is the responsibility of the HEI to cover the college's courses in its agreement. Where there is a recognised funding consortium, it is the responsibility of the lead institution to present its partners' arrangements.

In March 2005, the first list of accepted agreements was published on the Offa website and the full documents were posted. The great majority of HEIs chose to charge the full £3,000, but with a wide range of support for students and application of the agreements to partner colleges – indeed, relationships were often not addressed at all. At that point, only five colleges had published agreements. By July 2006 there were 46, some first applying to 2007–08

Offa recognised that the complex situation of colleges had not been addressed: many indirectly-funded colleges have multiple franchise partners, many directly-funded colleges also have franchise

HEI partners and/or are members of a consortium. Additionally, some HEIs who validate directly-funded provision take a view about the fee the college should charge.

Guidance on the compilation of access agreements and all the approved agreements are published on: www.offa.org.uk.

Access agreements should normally be submitted up to the beginning of January the year before they are due to take effect (i.e. January 2007 for 2008–9), but, given that some institutions (mainly colleges) chose not to charge variable fees in 2006–07, and in order to allow institutions to gauge the reaction of the market after the first intake under variable fees, Offa announced it would accept submissions for 2007–08 from colleges until 31 May 2006.

The grant to HEFCE from the DfES for 2006–07 has as a condition that the Council imposes as a condition of funding that institutions do not set fees in excess of the maximum if they have an access agreement in place, or of the basic amount if they do not, and that specified financial penalties be imposed for breach of the terms of an access agreement or of the relevant fee cap.

Considerations:

- Are clear systems in place to advise HE applicants on the application process, within the college or via an HEI partner(s), as appropriate, including eligibility, fees and financial support and the changes between 2005–06 and 2006–07 and on?
- Are courses listed in UCAS and are arrangements in place for responding to applications, including during the Clearing process?
- Are there clear systems for applying for support funding and for the relevant provision made under any access agreement from 2006–07, within the college or with a partner HEI as appropriate?
- Is agreed learning support accessible?
- Are the provisions of any access agreement (that of the college and/or partner(s)) clearly set out in marketing material covering the whole period of each course?

5 Partnerships and frameworks

This chapter looks at the types of partnerships that operate between colleges and higher education institutions in relation to their higher education provision and touches briefly on some other relevant partnerships. It recognises the increasing role partnerships have in some policy initiatives, their impact on HE providers and the challenges they pose for college management.

The issues will be of interest to:

- senior managers considering entering into new partnerships or reviewing their strategy for continuing existing links
- curriculum managers and HE coordinators operating or reviewing partnerships with HEIs
- staff from HEIs, who are responsible for collaboration and partnerships

The strategy for partnership

Along with historical legacy and opportunism, the strategic decisions behind FE/HE partnerships are usually made to offer niche vocational provision, provide local progression and a higher education experience for students who would not otherwise have one, for geographical reasons or to widen participation. Colleges have considerable experience of working with a range of vocational programmes, involving employers and work-based learning for part-time students, some of whom wish to obtain professional qualifications. It is still usually more difficult for people to study part-time in an HEI than in a college, so the flexibility of higher education in colleges can offer the partner HEI an additional opportunity.

Many of the students who enrol on such programmes require a good deal of support, especially at the early stages if they are returning to learn. The support that colleges offer all their students tends to be centrally organised, which can have funding implications when additional funding is not specifically funded for HEFCE-funded programmes as it is for those funded by the LSC. The availability and quality of such support has been acknowledged by the QAA and others as very important to 'second chance' students as they gradually become independent learners and see their potential for going further. The small groups, accessible tutors who frequently offer help at the point of need, as well as the central learning support services, are likely to make a difference to students from under-represented groups, or mature students whose confidence may need reassurance.

In terms of staff development, college staff have much to offer their HE colleagues in this and other areas, such as flexibility of delivery and work-based learning. They are also keen to increase their knowledge of higher education processes and scholarship. So some partnerships offer excellent staff development opportunities.

For colleges with relatively small higher education provision, working in partnership offers academic support, but also administrative support in terms of returns to HEFCE. Handing over the bureaucracy can be a real attraction for some colleges, while others prefer to maintain and manage their own systems.

Those partnerships developed out of mutual interest and enthusiasm, usually starting at course or curriculum level, generally tend to work well. In such cases, small groups of staff in HEIs and colleges develop, deliver and monitor a programme with widening participation as a common aim. At best, the relationship is one of mutual benefit and equality of function and purpose; at worst it can be paternalistic, patronizing or predatory, or a combination of all three. The *Review of indirect funding agreements and arrangements between higher education institutions and further education colleges* (HEFCE 03/57) highlighted examples of both of these types of partnership.

Partnership has become an increasingly important aspect of the way higher education is developed and delivered in further education colleges. A government steer in the White Paper, *The future of higher education*, in 2003 identified 'structured partnerships' as a way of ensuring quality in HE in FE. Before that, HEFCE introduced funding consortia in 1999 to supplement franchise arrangements and to extend partnership and collaboration and reduce administration for colleges. The primary difference between a consortium and a franchise relationship relates to the respective responsibilities of the institutions concerned. In a franchise partnership, the franchiser receiving the HEFCE funds is fully responsible for the students and accountable to HEFCE; a consortium, by contrast, is a partnership in which the funding flows through a lead institution but each partner retains responsibility and accountability for its own students. (See Appendix A.)

Regardless of whether their funding is direct or indirect, colleges commonly work in partnership with higher education institutions, other colleges in a consortium, employers, Sector Skills Councils (SSCs) and regional and sub-regional agencies within a range of arrangements, frequently dependent on the size and scale of the higher education in the college. Most partnerships are affected in some way by funding as described in Table 5.1 on page 81.

Types of partnership and networks

HE/FE partnerships have many elements in common but some features that relate to particular kinds of partnership. For example, partnerships operating over a period of time, in some cases 20 years or more, build up familiarity and trust. Some of these have developed into very close relationships, such as the college partnership which has become a faculty of the HEI. As in many other aspects of HE in FE, a strategic decision to enter into or continue a partnership in a changing environment affects the success of the partnership. The articulation of the strategy to all staff involved at all levels increases understanding and motivation. Some partnership decisions are made by senior managers without consulting the programme staff who will have to implement the decision, which can create difficulties. Others are historical arrangements which are not always reviewed regularly to ensure that they are still fit for purpose. Effective partnerships build a common knowledge, understanding and trust that cement future relationships. Any partnership takes time to develop and depends on a degree of commitment and shared objectives. New partners cannot expect a fully-formed partnership to take shape quickly.

Table 5.1 Types of partnership

Type of funding	Key features of funding arrangements
Direct funding	• The college draws down its own HEFCE funding. Its programmes are validated by one or more HEIs and/or Edexcel. • Where the programme is validated by an HEI, the HEI is responsible for the standards and quality of the award.
Indirect funding	• The HEI franchises a programme or part of a programme to an indirectly-funded college and uses its own HEFCE allocation of student numbers. • The HEI might develop the programme or work jointly. • Alternatively, the HEI validates a programme developed by a college but delivered with student numbers from the HEI. • Some HEIs operate a system of associate colleges for their indirectly-funded provision. Occasionally this is an exclusive relationship.
Funding consortia recognised by HEFCE	• Funding consortia were established in 1999 to allow groups of colleges to work together to use their allocated numbers more flexibly and to reduce the administrative burden by operating through one lead institution. • There are currently nine consortia, three of which are led by colleges.
More specific partnerships	
Progression partnerships	• Colleges have a range of partnerships that allow for progression from Access courses, or HNDs and Fds in arrangements that allow for one additional year to gain an honours degree (2+1) in an HEI or two additional years (2+2), • Some, like the Fd route, are agreed and articulated at the design stage. • Many of these are based largely on subject links, without extensive broader requirements.
Subject-based partnerships	• Large and small partnerships operate in one subject area, commonly teacher training. • This gives a particular coherence to curriculum development and planning. • Foundation year schemes frequently offer a subject base for progression.
University centres	• A number of HEIs have established structured partnerships with one or more colleges in a formal arrangement, which may be called a university centre or become one of the faculties of the university.
Lifelong Learning Networks (LLNs)	• LLNs are groups of at least two HEIs with colleges and other organisations brought together to promote vocational progression into and through higher education. • Introduced by HEFCE in 2004, the numbers of LLNs that have been awarded funding is steadily growing. • There is no one model, so there is a wide range of networks. • For further information, see the range of circular letters and progress reports on LLNs on the HEFCE web site: www.hefce.ac.uk/widening participation

Multiple partnerships

Colleges operating multiple partnerships may wish to expand their HE provision and combine direct and indirect funding, so that decisions are made according to the partner institutional strategy and the most appropriate academic links.

Concern is occasionally expressed that multiple partnerships place undue burdens and demands on colleges because of the different institutional practices and systems, particularly related to quality. For some colleges this impact is limited, partly because they have made a conscious choice to make these connections for good reasons and partly because the differences in systems are frequently quite superficial. The central relationship is at the subject level, which usually involves different staff teams in both institutions. It is important, nevertheless, for colleges to have detailed knowledge of how the HEIs work and how decisions are made. Problems can occur when colleges decide to work with a range of HE partners without fully understanding or making allowance for the increased work involved.

Although there are differences in practice between programme approval, validation and quality management and enhancement, a college with sufficient provision to sustain several relationships usually appoints a dedicated HE coordinator who becomes expert in the similarities and differences (for further detail, see Chapter 4). Size and scale make a considerable difference. Getting a grip on these matters has been made easier by the implementation of the QAA Academic Infrastructure (see Chapter 6). However, because so many of the areas of partnership are covered by the *Code of Practice for the assurance of academic standards and quality in higher education*, especially *Section 2: Collaborative Provision*, ways of operating have become more rather than less complex in recent years because of the expectations underpinning the quality of all HE provision.

The size and scope of partnerships

The typology of partnerships in Table 5.1 sets out some of the main partnerships. Within the descriptors is a range of arrangements which can be affected by scale among other factors. On the one hand, a college may have partnerships with several HEIs, perhaps because there is greater choice in a large conurbation or because the college is situated in a rural location where the nearest HEI cannot meet all its curriculum needs. On the other hand, an

HEI may franchise provision to a number of colleges in a series of bilateral arrangements or lead a consortium with several FE partners. These multiple partnerships can create additional work in terms of aligning quality systems, but the colleges involved commonly feel that the greater choice makes up for the burden.

A college with wholly franchised arrangements can be somewhat constrained as it may have little control over shifts of policy in the HEI and the college is not always able to plan strategically. In a consortium, decisions are more consensual and the colleges use their own quality assurance processes to monitor and enhance their HE provision.

Considerations:

- Who initiated the partnership and did all partners share the same reason?
- Has this position been reviewed as circumstances change?
- Are the values and purpose shared by all members of the partnership?
- How does the partnership deal with potential competition?
- What do students gain from the partnership to enhance their learning experience?

The impact of policy on partnership

Many government-led policies have urged partnership and collaboration bringing about the 'semi-compulsory' partnerships discussed in Chapter 2. Some recent funding initiatives have made partnership a central criterion, which has had mixed results. For example, the introduction of Foundation degrees in 2000 was dependent on partnership working. Even directly-funded colleges were not able to develop prototype Foundation degrees without a lead HEI and not only for purposes of validation. Subsequent bids in 2003 for additional student numbers were ring-fenced to Foundation degrees and HEIs were required to demonstrate that they had further education partners.

An earlier formulation of partnership policy was introduced by the HEFCE in 1999, when groups of colleges were invited to form funding consortia, led by one HEI or FEC. This initiative aimed to channel the allocation of student numbers through the lead institution, offering streamlined administration to the colleges (and less burden) and the flexibility to vire student numbers between institutions, some of which had very small HE numbers. Although driven by issues of administrative coherence, the funding consortia have added value to some partnerships by including curriculum and staff development and more coherent planning. In some cases, where institutional mission has changed, the consortia have lost members or disintegrated. The relatively small number of functioning consortia suggests that they work most effectively where there is only one HEI, which often means a regional setting with a limited number of HEIs. There are no longer any funding consortia in large conurbations.

A further example of partnership led by policy rests with the emerging Lifelong Learning Networks.

LLNs demonstrate another HEFCE/LSC policy that is predicated on partnership. The LLN initiative, while taking in other elements, is mainly aimed at securing progression to higher education as part of a 'Joint Progression Strategy'. Partnerships that form LLNs must include at least two HEIs, one of which should be a research-intensive university, together with colleges and a range of other stakeholder partners. It is not unusual for an LLN to have as many as 25 members, but all LLNs have their own specific approach to their partnership. Many are regional or sub-regional, but others are subject-based, for example, health or the arts. As they develop, some LLNs are forming informal partnerships with other LLNs to share ideas and practice.

As with Aimhigher in its early days, colleges have to declare an interest in the LLN and be prepared to commit time and work to progress it. Although there are usually far more college members in an LLN, the lead is commonly taken by HEIs.

Shortly after the publication of the 2006 FE White Paper, there were 22 fully-funded LLNs in operation. Collaboration and the expansion of the networks was flagged throughout the document. In addition, a new set of specialist networks driven by National Skills Academies and formed of effective specialist providers including colleges, CoVEs, specialist departments in HE and employers was proposed to support delivery and progression.

Conditions for an effective partnership: what makes it work?

The most successful partnerships usually concentrate on the student experience and the curriculum provided for their learning. A shared enthusiasm for a subject or for working with non-traditional students enables staff in HEIs and colleges to work together. Such collaborative work provides a setting for flexibility and innovation so that students have a learning experience that meets their needs. Underpinning this cooperation are a few elements that can make a significant difference to the implementation.

Long-standing partnerships, by definition, have built up the familiarity and trust that is the key to all successful partnerships. They demonstrate the way institutions grow into their relationships, adjust and change their operations and involve innovative and collaborative development. One or two of them have matured to the point where they are helpful models.

A university that has few regional competitors has a partnership of over 20 years' standing which won the Queen's Award in 1994. In 2005 it was awarded status as Centre of Excellence in Teaching & Learning (CETL) for HE in FE. There are 18 partner colleges with a total of over 3,500 full-time and over 2,000 part-time students on more than 300 programmes. In 2003 the university reviewed the relationship with the partner colleges by forming them into a new Faculty of the university. This unique development gives HE in FE equal standing with other faculties of the university, and provides a robust platform for strategy; shared responsibilities for quality assurance, marketing, planning; collaborative curriculum development; staff development and enhanced services for students.

> The CETL bid states that the partnership 'is based on our success in working together to improve the quality of student experience by developing staff, enhancing the infrastructure and sharing good practice'.

Indirectly-funded arrangements

Any indirectly-funded partnership benefits from having transparent arrangements – clear to all those involved, not only those at the most senior level. A system of regular, robust and clear communication helps to make the arrangements operate smoothly. The code of practice that HEFCE developed in 2000 offered guidance about indirect funding agreements and arrangements and is being revised so that it complements the section on collaborative provision in the QAA code of practice. The focus of HEFCE's revision is on funding but HEFCE also plans to work with the Higher Education Academy to gather and disseminate good practice in collaborative working.

Memorandum of collaboration

The memorandum of collaboration or partnership agreement is the formal framework by which the partnership operates. The project team that carried out the HEFCE review of indirect funding agreements and arrangements received over 500 documents, demonstrating a wide range of approaches. These followed a continuum from highly formal agreements in legalistic language at one end to much more user-friendly documents at the other that had concepts of partnership and collaboration firmly embedded.

It is necessary to cover the legal requirements of such an agreement; for example, what happens if there are serious financial problems or what happens to the students if the course needs to be withdrawn?

It is worth considering who should be party to the agreement. The HEFCE review found that in many colleges, the key people delivering the partnership outcomes had never seen the partnership agreement, let alone its financial schedule (HEFCE 03/57).

Successful partnerships are helped and supported if they are underpinned by a clear and transparent agreement.

Managing cultural difference

HEIs and colleges operate in a context with cultural differences: the range and background of students; the flexibility of provision and delivery; the range of staff and proportion of full-time to part-time staff (commonly 60:40 in colleges), and their conditions of service; funding sources; quality regimes; to list but a few. A successful partnership will take account of the differences and work together to agree common ground where it matters. In the early stages of a partnership, recognising any confusion created by the cultural difference will help to create effective ways of working.

Clarity of roles and responsibilities

It is extremely helpful to colleges and HEIs if all the roles and responsibilities of the partnership are clearly set out. From this information, college staff will be clear about their own responsibilities for nominating an external examiner, attending examination boards, agreeing marketing material and gaining access to the HEI's library resources. The HEI will also be able to set out requirements for quality procedures and their oversight, along with identifying their own responsibility for moderation of assessment, staff development and module modification. Most HEIs have link tutors who work at a practical level with the college to ensure that requirements are met.

This information can be very useful when set out as a list of roles, responsibilities and contacts to be shared by all partners. It can then be used as a basis for negotiating roles and staff development in the colleges, given the impact on FE staff of their contracts and conditions of service (see Chapter 7).

Following the QAA review of Foundation degrees in 2004–05, the overview report states:

Partnerships are also central to a high-quality Fds, and many of the programmes reviewed demonstrate strengths in these areas. Of particular note are the effective teamworking practices between staff from further education colleges (FECs) and their colleagues in higher education institutions (HEIs). These underpin effective collaboration through all phases of the programme and, for example, help to set and maintain consistent quality and standards across all partners within consortia. Partnerships with employers and employer representatives are highly developed in some programmes and this makes a significant contribution to the ongoing currency and viability of the Fd.

(QAA 2006: 2)

Funding transparency

Clarity and transparency about funding FE/HE partnerships can be critical to the success of the partnership, although in some these issues take second place to the curriculum offered to students. Few aspects challenge trust as much as funding. As autonomous organisations, HEIs have different costing models and calculate their funding for indirect funding arrangements in different ways. It is not always possible to deduce how these figures are derived and HEIs vary in the extent to which they are willing or able to explain.

This is understandably one of the major areas of difficulty and frustration for colleges. While many are appreciative of the partnership, they do not always believe they are getting value for money. HEFCE operates on the principle that the teaching grant funds students in subject areas at the same rate, so there is a perceived contradiction for colleges which receive 70 per cent of the funding of an HEI for the same programme without clearly being able to see what they get for the 30 per cent held back. On the other hand, HEIs point out that partnership work is time-consuming and expensive.

As it prepared to become a Lifelong Learning Network, one grouping addressed this issue with its partners for all new provision being designed for the LLN. The HEIs involved had different approaches, different costing models and varying levels of openness about their funding. A report considered very seriously by the LLN suggested looking at 'value' rather than 'costing'. By placing a percentage value on an activity (e.g. 7.5 per cent for validation and quality assurance and 45 per cent for teaching, learning and assessment), the LLN planned to achieve greater equality, transparency and coherence.

Considerations:

- How is the partnership maintained and sustained?
- Are all those involved in the partnership clear about their role and responsibilities?

- How do the partners ensure continuity of responsibility, especially in the face of staff changes?
- Do all partners understand how the funding is distributed and what it covers, and is there a mechanism for questioning the funding arrangements?
- How does the HEI ensure that quality and standards are consistently monitored throughout the partnership?
- What changes could be made to improve the partnership?

Some critical success factors for partnerships

- Strategic decision to form a partnership
- Openness and trust
- Awareness of sensitivities/politics
- Parity – partnership agreement
- Transparency of funding
- Clarity of roles and responsibilities
- Shared involvement in curriculum design and delivery
- Understanding of quality assurance and other arrangements
- Minimum burden
- Validation as enhancement
- Staff development (both HE and FE)
- Opportunities for scholarship and research

Working with other partners

Colleges are used to working with a variety of partners and many of those who will be useful to their HE provision will be partners they know already, like the Learning and Skills Council. Those listed below may lead to relationships that are positive for certain aspects of the HE provision:

Regional Development Agency: the RDA might house a number of partners who could help, notably the Regional Skills Partnerships, which can offer a helpful way in to making contact with employers. The RDA produces labour market intelligence which can inform HE curriculum planning although it is frequently too broad-based to be of significant value.

Learning and Skills Council: although the LSC only funds non-prescribed higher education, much of the provision funded at level 3 offers potential for progression from apprenticeships and Centres of Vocational Excellence. Each group of local LSCs in each region has a regional director to lead the strategy.

TUC Learning Services: the growing number of TUC learning representatives are enthusiastic about working with colleges to provide the education and training their members need. There is a good deal of potential for joint development work.

Sector Skills Councils: SSCs are now available for 25 sectors. They are at varying stages of development but all are encouraged to establish a Foundation degree Framework which partnerships can use to help plan a new Foundation degree. A few have chosen not to do this. SSCs operate as brokers between employers and HE providers and their Sector Skills Agreements are becoming increasingly important. They work closely with the Skills for Business Network and the Sector Skills Development Agency, which has regional managers.

Chamber of Commerce: the local Chamber will have direct contact with employers and colleges may be able to use their contact lists when they are developing Foundation degrees or other qualifications that involve employers.

6 Quality assurance, quality enhancement

This chapter addresses the regulatory and quality regimes applied to higher education in colleges as for prescribed and non-prescribed higher education and for directly- and indirectly-funded provision. The differences and similarities between the quality arrangements for higher and further education are an area of interest and occasionally concern for colleges, depending on their experience. The new method of review for colleges is described and explained. Particular reference is made to the Academic Infrastructure of the Quality Assurance Agency for Higher Education (QAA) and its role in providing core coherence to quality arrangements. The quality enhancement dimensions of assessment and review processes are emphasised, including annual course review, periodic review and peer review of teaching. The nature and role of validation, external examining and professional and statutory body accreditation are also discussed.

The issues will be of interest to:

- senior managers with responsibility for reviewing the higher education strategy
- senior managers responsible for quality assurance
- curriculum managers and HE coordinators responsible for the quality assurance procedures involved with their academic partnerships
- HE programme leaders
- staff responsible for academic partnership in awarding bodies.

Regulatory and quality regimes

Quality assurance arrangements for higher education present colleges with some challenges. The arrangements led by the QAA are different from those of Ofsted (previously in conjunction with the Adult Learning Inspectorate (ALI)) in some significant respects. On the other hand, when consulted by the quality agencies and others, many colleges have said that they believe the QAA systems offer useful and focused staff development in spite of the additional burden.

Current range of methods

The method of review or inspection depends largely on the source of funding of the provision, as described below.

Table 6.1 Sources of funding and processes of review

Directly funded HE provision in colleges	Provision that is validated by a higher education institution or by an awarding body, such as Edexcel, is reviewed in the college.
	QAA Academic review has taken place at the subject level, covering a range of programmes that matches a subject category.
	Academic review involves self-evaluation, a visit, usually of two days, and a published report once judgements have been made.
Indirectly funded provision in colleges	HE programmes delivered in colleges that receive indirect funding from an HEI are part of the HEI's institutional or collaborative audit. This covers franchised programmes or any programmes developed by a college but delivered through the HEI's allocation of student numbers.
	Being part of QAA audit may mean a much lighter scrutiny for the college. The documentation required and the amount of time (if any) spent on visiting the college is much less than for Academic review.
	This area of apparent disparity has been recognised in proposals for a new review method for colleges and is discussed below.
Directly or indirectly funded provision of Foundation degrees in colleges	QAA Foundation degree review operated in two discrete periods, 2002-03 and 2004-05. The validating HEI which was held responsible for the provision at the time of the review had overall responsibility for the review, which dealt with only one Fd programme at a time.
	Reports of both these review periods, a follow-up to the 2002–03 and a report on HNDs converted to Fds can be found on the QAA website, www.qaa.ac.uk

Table 6.1 Sources of funding and processes of review (continued)

HEFCE approved consortia	The review follows the Academic review process and focuses on a subject. The review is organised through the lead organisation (whether HE or FE) for all partners that deliver in that subject area.
Non-prescribed higher education (NPHE)	NPHE covers the 60,000 students (mostly part-time) studying professional qualifications in colleges or other programmes at levels 4–7 on the National Qualification Framework and funded by the LSC.
	They are accredited/validated and moderated by national awarding bodies.
	Any differences between these and other higher-level programmes funded by HEFCE are rooted in the funding source and create differences and difficulties.
	If these programmes are reviewed at all, and some are not, they come under the aegis of Ofsted (previously Ofsted/ALI) inspections which have a very different approach from QAA reviews.
National Health Service (NHS) provision	NHS provision (but not medicine and dentistry) is reviewed under a partnership arrangement consisting of all health professional organisations and the Workforce Development Confederation. NHS provision is now funded by the SSC Skills for Health.
	The QAA was commissioned to carry out major review of the health professions by the Department of Health with the Health Professions Council and professional bodies. It was a discrete method, also based on self-evaluation and visits, with visits to practitioner sites as well as teaching institutions.
	Fds in Skills for Health funded subjects form part of major review.
	A new model is being developed by Skills for Health. A composite report was published.
Professional Statutory and Regulatory Body (PSRB) accreditation	PSRB accreditation is an important requirement for various subjects and occupations (e.g. accountancy or the Allied Health Professions) and meeting the requirements, usually on a five-year cycle, is a source of additional work for institutions.
Training and Development Agency (TDA)	Any colleges that have TDA funding for their initial teacher training (ITT) for schools are liable to Ofsted inspection for ITT. This is a different branch of Ofsted with yet another framework. This method now also incorporates licence to practice and links to funding.

Given the range of quality assurance regimes during 2005–06, a single college with multiple partnerships and a range of prescribed and non-prescribed HE could have been subject to the following:

- QAA Academic review of art & design or of dance, drama and performance arts (HND, HNC, undergraduate, postgraduate). Depending on student numbers, these may have been combined into a single review and may have included Foundation degrees
- QAA institutional or collaborative audit (as a partner of the HEI being audited)
- QAA Major review (for their nursing provision as a partner of the lead HEI)
- a visit from a professional or statutory body and/or accreditation agency
- Ofsted/ALI full college inspection (with some non-prescribed level 4/5 programmes being inspected e.g. AAT, CIM, CIPD, NVQ, TESOL)
- TDA inspection of initial teacher training for schools

This list simply identifies the possibilities. It is extremely unlikely that all would coincide in any one year. In addition, all awarding bodies, including HEIs and Edexcel, have their own quality arrangements which must be followed by colleges offering programmes they validate.

Considerations:

- Is there someone in the college with an allocated responsibility for leading on whichever of these methods applies to the provision and keeping up-to-date with changes?
- Who has co-ordination and oversight of all of these methods?
- Where there are partnerships, are partner HEIs involved in advising or working collaboratively?

QAA review and further education inspections

Table 6.2 Comparison of QAA review and FE inspection

Activity	FE inspection (Ofsted)	QAA review
Similarities		
Self-evaluation	Both methods use self-evaluation and expect colleges to be open about their strengths and areas for development. Where issues are identified, it is expected that strategies should be in place or planned to deal with them. Both methods use data at the programme level and want to know how it is used for quality enhancement.	
Evidence base	Both methods expect evidence to support the self-evaluation/assessment	
Centrality of student work	Attention is paid to student work but because the inspection is carried out at a more macro level in the college, the scope and detail are not the same.	Scrutiny of student work is a key feature to inform curriculum design, teaching and learning and assessment. Archiving student work will make available the necessary range, along with unit outlines, learning outcomes and assessment.
College representative	The college nominee works with the inspection team and is an advocate for the college.	The subject review facilitator has a similar role but does not take part in discussions about judgements and is not an advocate.
Visit to the college	When the team is inspecting the whole college, the visit usually lasts a week. The revised system from 2005–06 allows for varying intensity according to track record.	Following a preliminary meeting to agree the arrangements, there are two further days: one initial meeting and one other day, usually within two weeks.
Management of the inspection/ review	There is a lead inspector who manages the review and ensures inspectors abide by the Ofsted code of practice. He or she is subject to scrutiny by the college and Ofsted. The local LSC, college managers and governing body are visited and given feedback during inspection.	Review coordinators, in a similar role, work on contract. Coordinators ensure the review follows the QAA code of practice and achieves a balance of activities in gathering robust evidence for judgements. There is likely to be involvement of/discussion with HEI subject partners or relevant college managers re: the review process.

Table 6.2 Comparison of QAA review and FE inspection (continued)

Activity	FE inspection (Ofsted)	QAA review
Lines of enquiry	The Common Inspection Framework (CIF) addresses areas of interest that are very similar to that of the QAA, although the focus may differ. For example, Ofsted benchmarks colleges against national benchmarks for retention and achievement.	The QAA concentrates on standards: intended learning outcomes, curriculum design and content, assessment, achievement and (under quality of learning opportunities) teaching and learning, student support and progression and learning resources. The maintenance and enhancement of quality and standards is an overarching area. The review relates to the provision in that college with a focus on subject areas; national comparisons are not made, but subject benchmark statements may be used as appropriate.
Differences		
Self-evaluation	The self-assessment is for the whole college and produced for the LSC as a self-assessment report (SAR).	The self-evaluation is about the subject and programme level so is more detailed at that level. A self-evaluation document is produced for each review.
Peer review	Ofsted employs both full-time and part-time inspectors. The regime is inspectorial.	QAA contracts but does not employ specialist subject reviewers, who are usually seconded from institutions and engaged in similar work. The philosophy of peer review is at the heart of QAA review.
Qualification frameworks	Where programmes inspected are in a qualifications framework, it is the National Qualifications Framework (NQF) administered by the Qualifications and Curriculum Authority (QCA). The higher levels 4–7 are equivalent to Intermediate level in the Framework for Higher Education Qualifications (FHEQ) (see Appendix A)	Higher education programmes are placed on the FHEQ, for example, Fd/HND at intermediate (I) level and honours degree at honours (H) level.

Table 6.2 Comparison of QAA review and FE inspection (continued)

Activity	FE inspection (Ofsted)	QAA review
Judgements	There is a numerical grade: 1 = Outstanding 2 = Good 3 = Satisfactory 4 = Inadequate for a curriculum area where inspected and a similar grade for crosscutting themes like leadership and management and student support. The 2006 FE White Paper proposes a new 'balanced scorecard' approach and judgements ranging from Excellent to Poor.	Numerical judgements ended in 2002. Judgements of confidence or no confidence are reached for standards. For the quality of learning opportunities, the judgements are commendable, approved or failing.
Teaching observations	It was standard to have a large number of teaching observations but under the revised method for 'good' colleges this includes only observations to verify the self-assessment.	Teaching observations only take place if there is insufficient evidence that there are sound systems to secure good quality teaching.

Colleges' perceptions of the similarities and differences

Colleges have seen some reduction in burden as the QAA methods have changed over the last few years. The peer review process enables them to check that they are taking account of the appropriate aspects of their provision and the preparation and review is a staff development opportunity that offers considerable enhancement.

The fact that provision is reviewed differently according to whether it is directly or indirectly funded means that the source of funding determines how the quality of provision is scrutinised. Because the awarding HEI is responsible for the quality and standards of any indirectly funded provision in colleges, it is quite possible for some programmes at the same level to be reviewed by the QAA (if they are directly funded) and for others at the same level (but indirectly funded) to have no external scrutiny at all outside the HEI's quality assurance systems. This has an effect on the college's ability to compare the standard of its higher education provision with that of an HEI. The new method proposed by the QAA for 2007–08 seeks to address this unevenness.

Considerations:

- Is the responsibility clear when it comes to preparing for different kinds of inspection or review in terms of producing the self-evaluation, preparing staff and collecting evidence?
- If a QAA review is to take place, will there be some administrative support and some time for staff teams to meet as part of their preparation?
- Has a system been agreed to archive students' work if it is to be needed for a QAA review?

The role of the QAA Academic Infrastructure

The QAA Academic Infrastructure, formerly known as external reference points, has been developing steadily over the past few years and enables colleges to have a firm grasp of what is expected of them. This is not to say that there is a set of rules or precepts where compliance is required. The Academic Infrastructure is a set of guidelines that underpins higher education to assure its quality and standards. It is worthwhile for curriculum managers and HE coordinators to be familiar with all aspects of the Infrastructure to ensure that their provision meets the requirements of higher education.

Academic Infrastructure

A summary of the main elements of the Academic Infrastructure is given in Table 6.3, followed by more detail.

Table 6.3 Elements of the Academic Infrastructure

Framework for Higher Education Qualifications (FHEQ)	Sets out the benchmark features and descriptors of qualifications at the levels within the FHEQ. Levels of award: 1 – Certificate (some HNC) 2 – Intermediate (Fd/HND, ordinary degree) 3 – Honours degree 4 – Masters 5 – Doctorate This framework maps across to the QCA National Qualification Framework levels 4–8 (see Appendix A).
Code of practice of the assurance of academic standards and quality in higher education	The code of practice that colleges should demonstrate they have addressed in their quality arrangements.
Programme specifications	The overview of how a programme is designed, delivered and assessed.
Subject benchmark statements	Benchmarks which draw together the threshold standards required for an honours degree in a particular subject.
Foundation Degree Qualification Benchmark (FDQB)	A generic set of statements about Foundation degrees that set out their defining characteristics.
Progress files	A transcript of student results and Personal Development Planning to reflect on progress. All institutions offering higher education should have had these in place from September 2005.
Teaching Quality Information	Information about provision, student achievement, external examiners' reports and other data required of HEIs on the HERO web site. Colleges joined the process later.

Framework for higher education qualifications

This framework enables colleges to place higher education awards at the appropriate level. Most are very clear: Foundation degrees and HNDs are at intermediate level and HNCs are commonly at intermediate level as well, although some are placed at certificate level. Honours degrees are at level H. Directly funded provision that is externally validated by a university will inevitably comply with the university's awards framework, which will in turn bear a relationship to the FHEQ.

A helpful aspect of the FHEQ lies in the lists of descriptors provided for each qualification. When designing or reviewing a programme, and especially when writing a programme specification, it is possible to check against the descriptors to ensure that the programme is being developed to the appropriate level. For example, it is possible that some programmes at intermediate level might not include an element in the curriculum that takes in the following phrases from the descriptor:

- applying underlying concepts and principles
- applying principles in an employment context
- evaluate critically different approaches
- critical analysis of information
- communicate to specialist and non-specialist audiences.

Code of practice for the assurance of academic standards and quality in higher education

The code of practice consists of ten sections covering such matters as collaborative provision, external examining, assessment, programme approval, monitoring and review, admissions, recruitment and placement learning. Each section is published as an A5 booklet or is available on the website and consists of a number of 'precepts'. The precepts are not regulations but come from collective good practice and can be used to help colleges ensure that they are working along the right lines. It can be helpful to take a set of precepts (say in Section 6: Assessment of Students) and use it as a staff development activity to determine what is already current practice and what can be improved. It is also useful to refer to knowledge of the code of practice in the QAA self-evaluation.

Programme specifications

Programme specifications were introduced to give staff, students and other interested parties an overview of the detail of a particular programme. Programme specifications can be produced in different ways, although a validating HEI might well expect a college to use their model. The specification covers such matters as the aims of the programmes, the learning outcomes, teaching and learning and assessment strategies, admissions and quality indicators. These are quite straightforward to prepare when the team producing the programme specification has designed the programme. When an off-the-shelf award is involved, like an HND, it takes more time to unpick the different elements of the programme.

In any QAA review, the programme specification is considered to be a vital piece of evidence.

The QAA publishes *Guidelines for preparing programme specifications* (available on the website and in the process of being reviewed), which set out all the minimum requirements for programme specifications and provides a number of templates of examples that go beyond the minimum. If colleges work closely with one or more HEIs, they may well have been given the templates the HEIs have devised, and indeed, if the HEI validates their programme, already be required to use them.

Progress files

The progress file consists of two elements: a transcript recording student achievement, which should follow a common format devised by institutions collectively through their representative bodies; and a means by which students can monitor, build and reflect upon their personal development.

Providers of higher education have gradually been developing transcripts of student achievement. Personal Development Planning (PDP) has also been introduced and it is expected that all providers had incorporated PDP from September 2005. PDP requires students to plan their learning and reflect upon it, but there is no one model. The QAA website gives guidance on all aspects of progress files. All providers of higher education are required to meet the European requirements for the Diploma Supplement, which gives a description of a student's programme, including the learning outcomes. The progress file should do this, but there are implications for colleges in terms of storing data.

Teaching Quality Information

When uniform QAA subject review was abandoned in 2001, there was concern that the public information formerly contained in QAA reports and available on the QAA website would no longer exist. In the interests of public information, the HEFCE decided that a special website would be established to hold a range of information from all HE institutions. FE colleges will be included in this process from 2007; initially using LSC data for directly funded colleges and presenting data on franchise provision on the college provider's part of the site (HEFCE circular letter 09/2006 gives details).

Using the Academic Infrastructure to enhance provision

Since the Academic Infrastructure underpins all methods of QAA review and audit, it can provide useful staff development, targeted at those staff teaching on higher education programmes. Using the code of practice and the subject benchmark statements when designing a new programme can help with the writing of the programme specification. Introducing a briefing for newly appointed external examiners alongside Sections 4 and 6 of the code of practice (external examining and assessment of students) will support a clear and robust system of external examining. Using the Academic Infrastructure as a reference point and a guide rather than as rules for compliance will allow for more consistent provision of higher education in colleges within and between institutions.

Considerations:

- Are all members of staff involved in higher education provision, including part-time staff, aware of the Academic Infrastructure and its impact on their work?
- Have arrangements been made to fill any gaps with staff development?

Proposed future arrangements for the quality assurance of higher education in colleges

Why is a distinctive system needed? This chapter has already highlighted some of the reasons why a distinctive system is needed for the review of HE in colleges, which include comparability, even scrutiny of direct and indirect funding and consortium funding, and the recognition of the roles and responsibilities of awarding bodies. It is generally believed that Ofsted and the QAA can achieve some commonality, but their significantly different approaches make it difficult for them to be combined. The QAA continues to treat HE in FE differently from HE in HEIs because of their contractual arrangement with HEFCE. The QAA approaches HEIs through audit on an institutional basis. Colleges have an institutional relationship with the LSC that makes it impossible for the QAA to treat them in the same way. The 2006 FE White Paper called for better links between the QAA and Ofsted.

Integrated quality and enhancement review (IQER)

The new method of review for colleges will have some distinctive differences from what happened until 2006. It draws on the Prime Minister's Office of Public Services Reform, which focuses on the customer perspective, on outcomes, the place of self-assessment and evidence-based judgement, value for money, continuous learning from practice and cooperation and joint reporting with other inspectorates.

IQER addresses many of the issues mentioned above by proposing a review method predicated on enhancement that deals with all HEFCE-funded higher education, whether it is directly, indirectly or consortium funded, and with no increase of burden for HEIs. In responding to requests from colleges, IQER retains peer review, parity of processes for colleges and HEIs and a risk-based approach to deciding the level of scrutiny in a college (according to track record). It will be piloted in 2006–07 and is expected to be fully operational from 2007–12 on a five-year cycle. Details of the review method can be found on the QAA website and include 'Annex D: The 24 steps of IQER' which covers the full five-year cycle. Table 6.4 on page 104 summarises.

IQER will ask three core questions about academic standards and the quality of learning opportunities. The QAA will be responsible for reporting on the accuracy, liability and frankness of Teaching Quality Information (see page 101). The core questions will be mapped to the Common Inspection Framework questions used by Ofsted in order to increase consistency.

What is new about the IQER method is its coordinated approach. All colleges will have their summative (SR) and developmental (DR) reviews within a five-year period, led by a QAA officer, managed by the same QAA review coordinator and with some continuity of the four reviewers. Self-evaluation and negotiation will be at the core and the approach sets out to build capacity through enhancement. Students will be involved and have the opportunity to make a written submission. The college will have one or two institutional nominees who will be common to both SR (summative review) and DR (developmental review) and

Table 6.4 Proposed elements of IQER

Periodic summative review (SR)	Institutional level review of college management of HE quality and standards, once between 2007 and 2012 (apart from a few pilot reviews).
Annual programme of formative HE developmental review (DR)	At least one DR in the five-year cycle between 2007 and 2012. The first area for developmental review will be student assessment, an area of provision in which there are issues for colleges and HEIs. Looking at assessment will form part of a strand of capacity building.
Regular internal review and evaluation of HE at the subject level	This includes annual monitoring reviews and reflection on all external review of HE in the subject by awarding bodies, employers, etc.
All components underpinned by the Academic Infrastructure	The HEI is always responsible for the standards of their awards.
Negotiated cycle of activities	The college will have the opportunity to negotiate and plan.
Reporting to provide feedback to colleges and awarding bodies	There will be a verbal report after DR and SR but only the SR report will be published.

will be full team members for DR. The amount of time spent on the review will be negotiated and there is an oral report from the review coordinator.

There will be an abridged method for colleges with fewer than 100 FTEs.

The intention is that enhancement will be central because of the direct involvement of the college in the planning and implementation of the review, and the continuity created by key members of the review.

Managing HE quality and standards in the college

Many college quality systems are appropriate to all programmes whatever the level and can be used or adjusted effectively for HE provision. There are, however, some areas which benefit from some differentiation if the quality assurance is to be robust enough to meet the requirements of awarding bodies and the QAA. Those colleges that make a member of staff specifically responsible for higher education quality matters, albeit working closely with the

Table 6.5 Quality assurance roles and responsibilities

Awarding bodies	Any college developing a new HE programme will have to work with an awarding body, usually Edexcel or an HEI. In the case of a franchised programme, the development work may well have been completed but there will still be a need to prepare for validation. Awarding bodies have their own systems for validation but have many elements in common:
	Institutional review: some HEIs carry out an institutional review of the college's central systems, for example, finance, management, quality and learning resources. An overall review, which usually involves a panel visit, will then agree the core of the partnership and the subject-specific validation will accept those elements as given.
	Essential documentation: the range of what is required will almost certainly include, as a minimum, an assessment of market demand, a programme specification and a student handbook in addition to module or unit outlines with credits. The composition of the panel will usually be laid down by the HEI and will include an external adviser and probably, in the case of Foundation degrees, an employer.
	The FdF *National Validation Service Handbook* (2005) includes useful advice on validation, which can also be applied to programmes other than Foundation degrees.
	Professional accreditation: Professional, Statutory and Regulatory Bodies (PSRBs) also require the preparation of documentation and a panel visit to accredit a professional qualification and will provide guidelines. Although there is a good deal of variation in the content and presentation of these documents, if core documents are held centrally with an allocated responsibility, it is much easier to use and adapt them.
Programme approval	Indirectly funded provision will automatically go through the awarding body procedures, whether it is an HEI or a national awarding body like Edexcel. There are considerable differences between them and it is helpful for each college to have its own coordinated scheme for programme approval to ensure that all elements are being met. For staff new to these procedures, sitting on a panel helps their staff development.
	Programme approval, especially of Foundation degrees, may include a market research exercise to ensure that there is both employer and student demand for a new programme. If the provision is vocational, evidence of employer involvement in the design and delivery of the Fd will reassure college staff that they are proposing something that is needed.
	Designing the programme and its specification with a view to the learning outcomes, credits, level of work and teaching, learning and assessment strategies are an important phase of programme development and involving HE colleagues can be very helpful.
	Section 7 of the QAA *Code of practice: Programme approval, monitoring and review* sets out very clearly what needs to be done and how colleges can approach this area.

Table 6.5 Quality assurance roles and responsibilities (continued)

Annual monitoring report/self-assessment	Colleges have become used to preparing self-assessments as part of continuous improvement that are used by the LSC and Ofsted. At programme level, these may not be very detailed, depending on centrally held data and sometimes tick boxes. Some HEIs also require a limited amount of detail for their equivalent of annual monitoring reports.
	Producing a more reflective, evaluative annual programme review offers the potential for the programme team to work together and produce a review that is enhancing, that makes them question what works well and what needs to be improved. Some colleges use the headings of core questions of a QAA self-evaluation as the basic template so that there is a more coordinated approach when they come to need it.
Periodic review	Most HEIs have a system that reviews programmes every five years. The period can be less, especially in the case of a new programme, as was the case with many Foundation degrees.
	An internal college review can be a tool for enhancement by involving staff in some streamlined preparation and thinking in preparation, and having a panel of subject and other HE staff in the college and an external adviser. As long as the review is carried out with a fairly light touch and to a tight timescale (one day is usually enough), a great deal can be gained.

college quality manager, probably get the results that are most fit for purpose. This section concentrates on those elements of quality assurance that may need special attention, with a view to adding value by enhancement.

Whether the college is directly or indirectly funded, it makes a real difference if the people involved with initiating or monitoring aspects of quality assurance know who they are and what they have to do. In the best indirectly funded partnership agreements, roles and responsibilities are clearly laid out, with the differing roles of the HEI and college effectively demarcated. This is particularly important when the provision of higher education is small (fewer than 100 FTEs) because it is possible for important aspects to slip through the net.

Chapter 3 examined organisation and managerial responsibilities; the specific responsibilities in relation to quality assurance include:

- intended learning outcomes (ILOs)
- module credit systems

- APEL and credit transfer
- assessment and verification or moderation (internal and external)
- examination boards and external examiners
- support for students
- Personal Development Planning (PDP)
- access to appropriate learning resources
- opportunities for student feedback and evaluation
- annual monitoring reports/self-assessment
- periodic review of programmes
- approval and validation of new programmes

Quality enhancement

Throughout this chapter, there have been references to enhancement and the ways in which quality assurance systems can enhance learning and the experience of the teaching staff. Many colleges have found that introducing new quality processes for their higher education or preparing for and participating in a QAA review is a form of enhancing their staff development; under IQER, enhancement is a thread that runs through everything.

Considerations

- Has there been an audit of where the quality systems described in the section above are similar or where they are different from FE systems?
- Where they are different, has the responsibility to ensure their effectiveness been allocated?
- Is there training for HE programme leaders and staff teams to ensure that they understand what they need to do?

7 Working with the curriculum

In this chapter we explore the ways in which developing and delivering a higher education programme in a college is subject to a number of internal and external pressures. Colleges do not have total ownership of their curricula, whether they are directly or indirectly funded, and whether they design their own programme or deliver one off-the-shelf. We look at teaching, learning and the student experience of higher education in a college and the support offered to students. We also discuss some of the features of a higher education environment and how this is implemented in colleges, integrated with their FE provision or provided separately.

The issues will be of interest to:

- senior managers with responsibility for curriculum development, student and learning support and resources
- curriculum managers and HE coordinators responsible for curriculum delivery
- programme leaders who manage higher education programmes
- student services staff responsible for supporting students
- staff responsible for learning resources and information technology
- link tutors in HEIs responsible for advising on existing programmes and developing new curricula

The nature of higher education in colleges

The notion of a higher education 'ethos' is frequently articulated, but it is captured in a variety of ways and not usually in a way that gives substance to what is meant by the term. One of the implications of using the notion of ethos is that it assumes an idea of homogeneity and a sense that all students in higher education receive or should receive the same experience. This cannot be true. In some senses, a small cohort studying HE in a college may have more in common with a one-to-one tutorial system still operating at an old university than with a large group of 200 students studying a popular subject in a newer university.

Any definition of what puts the 'higher' into higher education is elusive. The small-scale study carried out by the Learning and Skills Development Agency, *Dimensions of Difference*, lends support to 'the idea that HE in FE is a hybrid, in some ways more akin to further education and in other respects more like higher education' (LSDA 2003: 22). The bulletin identified the 'fragility of many of the claims to difference and distinctiveness' (2003: 21). For this reason, some of the ideas and expectations outlined below will apply differently to colleges, dependent on their mission, strategy, location and the size of their HE provision.

Designing the curriculum

A college's provision may comprise a limited number of discrete courses developed in relative isolation from each other, or a comprehensive set of programmes operating within a common set of arrangements; possibly a credit framework and credit accumulation and transfer (CAT) system. Chapter 3 examined the range of organisational arrangements and responsibilities and Chapter 5 highlighted the importance of partnership working at strategic and operational levels.

College curriculum teams become involved in developing or adopting curricula in several ways (outlined below). There is a spectrum of curriculum creation that has at one end the development of a whole programme in the college and, at the other, taking and delivering a ready-made programme. Whichever method is used, there are a number of key questions that need to be answered in the early stages of deciding on new curricula or reviewing existing programmes. Until fairly recently, it was common practice in both colleges and HEIs for an enthusiastic member of staff with an interest and expertise in a particular sector, subject or discipline to suggest designing a new programme. Some such ideas have been developed without any sense of market or student demand and it can be very dispiriting for a curriculum developer to be left with a course which nobody wants and which does not run. There were a number of examples of this with the very rapid introduction of Foundation degrees in 2001–02.

Preliminary planning questions which should be addressed before any curriculum design work starts include:

- Has there been any market testing to see whether there is a demand?
- If the programme is vocational, does it meet the regional skills priorities and have the support of the relevant Sector Skills Council (SSC) and some local employers who might support it?
- Is it likely to provide a progression route for level 3 students in the college, from a CoVE or from provision in other colleges and schools nearby?
- If there is a demand and the programme is developed, will there be any HEFCE student places available either through direct funding to the college or through a local HEI with spare numbers? (There are still cases of colleges wishing to embark on HE provision who are not aware of the need to secure HEFCE funded places.)
- Is the staff team qualified to deliver a higher education programme?
- Are there sufficient accommodation and learning resources to support the programme?

These questions, or questions like them, will frequently form part of a college or HEI programme approval system.

A spectrum of curriculum development models

Below we summarise the spectrum of curriculum development and the degree of control over the curriculum held by the college.

It should be noted that, in the context of curriculum development, the term 'franchise' is used to refer to the arrangement whereby an HEI franchises one or more colleges to deliver a programme of the HEI, and that collaborative arrangements for development and delivery may be described as a 'consortium' without being an HEFCE recognised funding consortium (see Appendix A).

Table 7.1 Models of curriculum development

College develops the curriculum and takes it to an HEI for validation	If the HEI accepts the programme with little question, this is the point on this spectrum which gives the college most control. This may not always be an advantage, for example in cases where an HEI validates a college programme in a curriculum area they do not offer themselves. The HEI is responsible for the standards of the programme, but may not have the subject expertise to ensure its quality.
College develops the curriculum in partnership with other colleges and then seeks validation	An early approach to the HEI validating partner may save time and developmental effort. Colleges working collaboratively can divide up the development work usefully as long as they meet and communicate and share the same values for the programme.
College develops the curriculum in partnership with an HEI, employers, the SSC and other colleges and organisations	This model is becoming more common as demand-led development gains favour. Early discussions can be very helpful even if most of the design work is then carried out by the college(s) – testing the detail as it is developed. Many Fds have been developed and are delivered in collaborative consortia.
College adopts an off-the-shelf programme from an awarding body such as Edexcel or a professional body	HND and HNC programmes are available off-the-shelf and still offer the opportunity for colleges to design up to two of their own units in order to include local factors. Apart from that option, the learning outcomes are laid down, although there will be considerable scope to develop teaching, learning and assessment strategies. Programmes that come under the heading of non-prescribed higher education, such as some awarded by professional bodies, will have their own systems and regulations.
College agrees to deliver a programme designed by an HEI as a franchise	An HEI offers a college the opportunity to deliver all or part of an existing programme which has been developed by the HEI curriculum team. The college is unlikely to have any input into the design until the programme is being reviewed but, as with the off-the-shelf example above, the college team will be able to use teaching, learning and assessment strategies that match the definitive document and programme specification.
College works with an employer to develop an employer-led programme	An employer, usually a large public sector employer like the Health Service or a local authority, or a private sector employer, works in partnership with a college and an HEI to develop a Foundation degree or other programme that will meet the needs of their workforce development.

Essential features and support to consider when designing a programme

Ascertaining demand

As has been stated above, there has been a gradual movement from developing new programmes out of interest and enthusiasm to a need to demonstrate that there will be a demand once the programme has been developed. For vocational programmes like Foundation degrees and higher nationals, demonstrating student demand is not sufficient. There needs to be an indication that the programme will meet local or regional needs and that the sector supports the development. Labour market intelligence from the Regional Development Agency (RDA), the LSC and the relevant SSC should enable the college to test need.

Place of employers/agencies

However, need and demand are not the same thing and skills priorities are sometimes aggregated to too broad a level to be useful locally. There may be a regional need for skills that employers do not see as important. Engaging employers in the development of new programmes is not easy, but there are a number of ways of gaining specific support or, indeed, recognising the need to think again. Contacting the local Chamber of Commerce, the regional directions for Foundation Degree Forward, the Skills for Business Network and the individual SSCs may help a curriculum team gain more information.

Cognitive and intellectual skills

In its latest report on *Learning from higher education in further education colleges in England 2003–05* (2006), the QAA draws attention to the need to develop further students' cognitive and intellectual skills. This may be discussed with a partner HEI to share practice or by looking closely at the level descriptors for intermediate level and honours levels qualifications in the Framework for Higher Education Qualifications (FHEQ).

It is essential to check that the curriculum design and intended learning outcomes offer students the opportunity to achieve those descriptors as an integrated part of their programme. It is possible that some relatively minor adjustments will make the programme more of a higher level experience.

Subject or qualification benchmark statement

The QAA publishes subject benchmark statements, and one qualification benchmark statement for the Foundation Degree (FDQB),
as 'reference points' for curriculum teams about threshold standards
for their programmes.

The subject statements have been derived from the academic
community in that subject, so they differ to some extent, which raises
issues for inter-disciplinary programmes. The subject benchmark
statements apply largely to honours degree programmes; this means
that they cannot simply be applied to higher nationals. However,
because so many HND/HNC and Foundation degree students
progress to complete an honours degree, staff in colleges can
usefully check their programmes against the subject benchmark
statements to ensure that students are adequately prepared for
progression.

The FDQB covers the generic, and distinctive, design characteristics of the qualification, specifying work-based outcomes in
addition to those of the Intermediate level of the FHEQ.

Determining accreditation of prior learning (APL)

Since so many students taking HE programmes in colleges are
mature students, curriculum teams need a policy about how to
acknowledge the accreditation of prior learning (APL) that would
give entry to, exemption or advanced standing on a higher education
programme. This may be prior certificated learning (APCL), recognising qualifications or parts of qualifications. Alternatively, the
work or life experience of the student may lead to the accreditation of experiential learning (APEL) or learning and achievement
(APL&A). A college working in partnership with an HEI will use
their systems, but this is a complex area and deserves early consideration. The QAA issued guidelines for APL in 2004.

Considerations:

- Has it been established that there is a clear demand for the
  programme to be delivered – both skills/employer demand
  and student demand?
- Will the college be able to get direct or indirect funding
  for the new programme?

- Is the staff team large enough and appropriately qualified?
- Are there sufficient resources in the college for quality to be ensured?
- Is there an effective partnership for any collaborative development?
- Is the validating HEI, if there is one, involved in the design and development?

Teaching, learning and the student experience

A central feature to be addressed by colleges in designing and delivering higher education is the need to create an appropriate HE environment and to address the 'higherness' of the programmes and of the student experience.

As indicated above, curriculum design is influenced by a range of external factors which will inhibit the extent to which a college can tailor make (rather than take) its curriculum. Where programmes are delivered in partnership with an HEI, the degree to which the college has control over the curriculum delivery, teaching and learning and assessment varies. In some cases, particularly where the same programme is delivered in the HEI, the HEI specifies not only the learning outcomes, but also the detail of module content and delivery, and the assessment schedule and tools.

Where the college has a level of autonomy, curriculum delivery will also be affected by financial considerations and by philosophical drivers or pragmatic decisions about the advantages of discrete or embedded provision (see Chapter 3). Teaching and learning strategies employed may be designed to mirror those of a partner HEI or may, at least in the early part of the programme, be designed to support a particular client group, including: mature student returners, students progressing from in-house Access courses, students progressing through specialist vocational programmes, younger 'gifted and talented' students on level 3 provision studying HE modules and, of course, students on part-time programmes and work-based Foundation degrees. In these cases, particular attention needs to be given to variety in teaching and learning strategies and to formative assessment underpinning summative assessment.

Where a programme is delivered by a range of FE partners in a consortium (as is increasingly common for Foundation degrees), particular attention needs to be given to consistency in delivery, standards and outcomes.

The academic environment

Students who progress from level 3 programmes to higher education usually notice a step change in the way they are expected to organise their study and produce work for assessment. A carefully structured induction that includes some of the key study skills helps them to adjust and is essential for mature students returning to learn after some time; reinforcement of these skills throughout the first year will help students make the transition to higher level study. We describe in Table 7.2, over page some of the important elements and sources of support for staff as they plan this underpinning study.

HE delivered in FE is more likely to follow the model of (small) classroom teaching than that of many universities where large lectures are the norm accompanied by variable amounts of small seminars or tutorials. While the number of hours of teaching tends to be higher in FE, there will be financial restrictions on allocated teacher hours and, particularly where provision is limited in volume, combinations of cohorts into lectures for common elements of unitised or credit-based programmes can allow release of more support time. This can then be used to compile the Progress Files, providing a transcript of student results and Personal Development Planning to reflect on progress, which have been a requirement since September 2005.

Course handbooks

Course handbooks covering the content, delivery and management of a course are standard practice and colleges often have a template for their production: but higher education programmes will require additional features. Where a course is delivered in partnership with an HEI, the format and varying amounts of the content are likely to be determined by the HEI.

Table 7.2 Aspects of higher education programmes

Higher-level skills	
Critical analysis and academic discourse	Some FE staff are very familiar with explicit level descriptors which identify the characteristics of the level of study, others are less so. The need for appropriate evaluation, analysis and presentation to agreed conventions are central to 'higherness' and will be spelled out in the qualifications framework and subject benchmarks (see below).
Working towards independent study and coping with challenge	A structured approach to becoming a reflective practitioner and an independent learner will take account of some of the examples listed below but will also depend on the curriculum design, the discipline and the teaching and learning styles adopted. Higher education students need to be able to meet the challenge of intellectual rigour.
Research and using source material	Higher level skills require the demonstration of knowledge generation through planned and reported research. Students who are progressing from a level 3 programme that did not include such a requirement (or who do not have a level 3 qualification) will need guidance in the initial stages about how to make most effective use of the Internet and other sources and about conventions of presentation within a discipline.
Referencing	A perennial problem for all higher education students, not simply using accurate referencing but understanding the need to acknowledge others' work.
Plagiarism	Connected with use of the Internet and with referencing, plagiarism is a growing problem. Colleges need to have a published policy and enforce any regulations. Programmes validated by an HEI will need to comply with that institution's plagiarism policy.
Assessment deadlines	Progressing students may not have been subject to rigorous enforcement of deadlines. It is one of the step changes for FE students progressing to HE and can become one of the elements that demonstrates the difference.
Progression	Much of the provision of HE in FE is 'Intermediate' level and, for these programmes, preparation for progression to an honours degree may be an integral aspect. Particular attention needs to be given to this if the honours degree is provided in a different mode of study. Progression routes from Fds should be established when the degree is validated and awarding institutions normally guarantee progression to at least one honours degree with the expectation that this should not normally exceed 1.3 years full-time. Other 'bridging' arrangements need to be considered.

Table 7.2 Aspects of higher education programmes (continued)

e-learning	Distance learning supported by email and virtual learning environments (VLE) is particularly appropriate for the part-time learners commonly found in HE in FE, particularly those following a work-based programme. Blended learning combines online learning with face-to-face teaching contact.
The QAA Academic Infrastructure	
The framework for higher education qualifications (FHEQ)	The generic descriptors and outcomes listed for each level of qualification in the FHEQ can be a useful way of checking that appropriate standards are being reached (see above). The National Qualification Framework (NQF) of the QCA is aligned to the FHEQ from levels 4–8 (see Appendix A).
Subject benchmark statements	Similarly, judicious use of the specific subject benchmark statements for particular disciplines (although set at the threshold of the honours degree) can be very useful when preparing Intermediate level students to progress onto a 2+1 or 2+2 programme.
Personal development planning (PDP)	Now part of the Academic Infrastructure, PDP combines the potential for a learning contract with reflective practice. When carefully designed, PDP operates at noticeably higher levels
Vocational qualifications	
Integrating academic and vocational learning	Many students in colleges are studying vocational programmes. Integrating the academic and vocational so that students can analyse and reflect on their practice adds value to their learning. This is one of the key defining characteristics of the Foundation degree and is central to that award.
Work-based learning (WBL)	This integration affects WBL in particular and moves it from the lower-level competence training done in colleges to applied learning that uses the workplace as one of its resources. Peer and experiential learning can play a significant role. The FDQB specifies outcomes that holders of Fds should be able to demonstrate.
Relevant guidance is set out in the QAA Academic Infrastructure: qaa.ac.uk/academic infrastructure	

The handbook should set out the programme specifications, which are a concise description of the intended learning outcomes (ILOs) and the means by which these outcomes are achieved and demonstrated.

It should reflect the elements listed in Table 7.2 above, including agreed conventions for referencing and bibliographies, assessment criteria and deadlines and a clear statement about plagiarism – recent court cases suggest that a signed statement that the student has received and understood guidance is necessary.

Assessment regulations and awarding processes should be set out in detail in line with the requirements of the awarding HEI or examination board.

In addition to being a comprehensive reference for the students on the programme, the handbook will operate as an introduction and guide for external examiners appointed by the awarding body and for QAA reviewers, as well as an induction and staff development tool for team members.

It is likely that information about content, reading lists and assessment will need to be set out by module. If courses include more than one level of certification and map to different levels of the FHEQ, this should be explicitly addressed at module level. In many cases, a separate module handbook is provided.

Student support
The student life cycle and progress through the institution needs specialist support from pre-application, through application, induction and on-course academic and pastoral support, including financial guidance, in order to enhance performance and retention.

As noted in Chapter 4, the HEFCE funding methodology does not support individual additional learning support in the same way as that of the LSC. Consequently, individual learning support (other than that funded through the Disabled Students Allowance) needs to be included within tutorial support. Academic support provided through learning centres or resource rooms should ideally be dedicated and funded via the amount of capital funding which is now available either to directly funded colleges or via HEI partners. Colleges with local partner HEIs are often able to benefit from arrangements allowing students access to the HEI's facilities.

Student feedback and progression

Students' perceptions of their experience are an integral part of the quality assurance regimes of both FE and HE (see chapter 6). Programme leaders collect information from students using a range of methods and external examiners may sample the views of students directly. The QAA revised process for HEI institutional audit enhances student participation in line with HEFCE recommendations and this will apply to HE in FE through IQER, so it is advisable to have a substantive body of evidence of students' responses to their experience and to use this to inform course review and updating and to support quality enhancement.

Colleges are not part of the First Destination survey carried out for other HE students by HESA. However, there are occasions when colleges are expected to report on progression, notably in QAA review. It is worth having a mechanism for tracking students' progress once they have completed. Some colleges do this by email, by telephone follow-up, by reunion occasions or by an alumni association.

Employer liaison

With the increasing policy emphasis on the development of higher level skills (in particular for colleges at intermediate/ technician level), employer involvement in curriculum development is important. Employers can play a central role in early discussions about need and demand but also engage in the design and development of a programme. In the case of Foundation degrees, the QAA review in 2004–05 cited good practice in a wide range of employer contributions, including the design of briefs and projects, student support (including mentoring) and assessment. While the challenge of maintaining an effective level of employer engagement was recognised, it is viewed as an enhancement of the currency and credibility of the qualification.

Considerations:

- Does the delivery of the programme ensure that higher level skills and knowledge are developed to relevant benchmarks and standards?
- Do teaching and learning styles meet the needs of the client group(s)?
- If progression to an honours degree is a planned outcome, are students prepared?
- Are all elements of programme delivery and assessment clearly documented?
- Are mechanisms in place to ensure that PDP is recorded?
- Is HE-specific student support in place?
- Are student perceptions of their experience systematically collected, reported and acted on?
- Are employers' views sought and employer liaison meetings held?

Staff development and scholarly activity

Conditions of service

Evidence suggests that the significant majority (if not all) of HE in FE is delivered under the same contractual conditions as FE in FE, even where staff teach only on higher education programmes. However, while teaching loads for staff teaching HE in FE may be higher than in an HEI, the amount of teaching and tutorial time allocated to HE programmes in FE is generally higher than those in HEIs while the group sizes are smaller, reflecting a prevalent perception that HE in FE should be and is distinctive – more locally based – and, with a client group who need greater support (at least initially). Staff may well be part-time, particularly on vocational and specialist programmes where recent employment sector expertise is important. A negative aspect of this can be lack of time to integrate the team members, particularly when the programme is delivered across a consortium.

Some staff teams are very small, with only two or three people having an input into the programme. This may not allow for a sufficient range of expertise to challenge students. HEIs have their own regulations about the level of qualification required of staff teaching on their validated programmes but a useful rule of thumb is that staff should be qualified to the level above that which they are teaching, i.e. someone teaching on an honours degree programme should have a master's award. An exception is commonly made on vocational programmes for someone with recent and relevant industrial experience.

Initial training and continuous professional development

Under the *Success for All* reforms, FE staff are required to have a teaching qualification. Bachelor of Education (BEd), Post-Graduate Certificate of Education (PGCE) and Certificate of Education (Cert.Ed) qualifications gained before September 2001 are recognised for the purposes of qualification: all other staff are expected to achieve a level 4 qualification endorsed by the Sector Skills Council (Further Education National Training Organization, FENTO, now replaced by Lifelong Learning UK (LLUK)) against targets by 2010. LLUK is taking forward reform of these standards and consultation will complete in 2006, with a new framework structure in place in 2007 covering teachers, tutors and trainers leading to a benchmark qualification Qualified Teacher/Tutor/Trainer in the Learning and Skills Sector (QTLS). The 2006 FE White Paper has reinforced these proposals and in September 2007 a new regulatory CPD requirement will be introduced.

In line with proposals in *The Future of Higher Education*, new staff in HEIs are expected to undergo initial training and continuous professional development. The Higher Education Academy accredits HEIs' programmes of training in teaching and learning and provides a service registering accredited practitioners. It led on the development of a standards framework for teaching and supporting student learning in higher education at the request of the UK funding councils for higher education, Universities UK (UUK) and the Standing Conference of Principals (SCOP) and, after two years of consultation, these were launched in February 2006. HEIs working in partnership with colleges may involve college staff in their programmes.

Decisions about whether staff specialise in higher education or teach across levels in a subject domain both affect and reflect decisions about the organisation and management of higher education provision. In colleges where provision is limited, it may simply not be an option to differentiate staffing; in others – both smaller and larger providers – it reflects perceptions as to whether the 'higherness' of the provision and the nature of the client group is distinctive or whether the higher education programmes and client group have more in common with level 3 provision (including Access to HE), and/or the salience of the vocational and work-related nature of the provision. Whatever the model, there will be a need for specific staff development to address the particularities of the funding and quality assurance systems as well as for subject or profession-specific updating. The Higher Education Academy, through its senior HE in FE Adviser, has appointed staff from FE colleges to work with subject centres on a part-time basis and undertakes in research into HE in FE, including a project on HE 'ethos'.

The HEFCE development fund was used by many directly funded colleges to reduce teaching hours against contract, and the funds for rewarding and developing staff can now be used in the same way. Such reduction is limited and does not usually release time for scholarly activity and activities such as QAA reviewing or external examining. When the development funds were mainstreamed it may have become less transparent to managers with the responsibility to develop the curriculum and enhance the delivery of higher education programmes what funding was available for the purpose. However, from 2006–07 (to 2008–09) a new Teaching Quality Enhancement Fund (TQEF) will support developments in teaching and learning. The fund is allocated in three strands: to support learning and teaching strategies and professional standards, for research-informed teaching and (unavailable to colleges) for volunteering activities in the community. The funds for research-informed teaching are being allocated in inverse proportion to research funding in order to support institutions without a strong research base. Colleges with over 100 directly funded FTEs are included in these arrangements and, for 2006–07, will receive funds ranging from around £4,000 to over £105,000.

Where colleges are indirectly funded they are entitled to access this (and other funding streams) through the franchising HEI. The HEI's plans should reflect capital and non-capital quality enhancement activities with and in its college partners and ensure that its own students and HE students in partner colleges receive a proportionate benefit from the TQEF. This is a matter that should be addressed in the compilation and review of partnership funding agreements.

> The staff who teach on HE programmes in colleges, particularly the large numbers of part-time staff and practitioners, will not always have the opportunity for the continuous academic debate and discussion that might happen in HEI staff rooms and meetings. A staff development strategy for higher education might include such matters as:
>
> - funded (or partially funded) opportunities to take higher degrees
> - getting involved with research with colleagues in other institutions
> - working with the Higher Education Academy subject centres
> - work-shadowing a colleague in an HEI
> - inviting a peer in another institution to be a mentor
> - putting on specific events to meet specific needs; assessment, work-based learning
> - ensuring that staff understand the QAA Academic Infrastructure through events and other practice; the new method of review, IQER, is predicated on the Academic Infrastructure being in place (see Chapter 6)
> - offering opportunities for industrial secondments
> - encouraging and supporting staff to become external examiners and/or QAA reviewers.

External examining and QAA reviewing offer excellent professional development opportunities. Edexcel requires external examiners employed to examine the directly accredited higher nationals to attend training events, and some of these examiners are staff involved in teaching and/or managing HE in FE. However, across HEIs franchising HNs under licence and validating Foundation or honours degrees, practice is more variable. There is little evidence of recruitment of FE-based staff as examiners and induction and training may not be provided. However, there are instances where strong partnerships have looked to FE, particularly for examiners for intermediate level work, and Fdf is supporting a database and network, and the Higher Education Academy has a research and support programme for externals. The QAA is committed to including FE-based staff in its review processes. In order to benefit from the developmental opportunities involved in examining and reviewing, staff need to be given managerial support and to have the activity formally recognised as a career development and as a form of scholarly activity.

Scholarly activity
The FENTO standards (currently being updated by LLUK) required staff to engage in continuing professional development, including engaging in research and study relating to their professional practice. The HE standards framework is committed to acknowledging the distinctive nature of teaching in higher education and recognising the autonomy of HEIs and of QAA's requirement that relevant research and scholarship be embodied in teaching. As indicated in Chapter 4, directly funded colleges cannot access research funding and thus are not subject to scrutiny of research activity. Some colleges do have a formal policy to encourage research (for both HE and FE engaged staff). Institutions and individuals have been active in the (then) LSDA Learning and Skills Research Network (LSRN), and the ESRC Teaching and Learning Research Programme with its emphasis on practitioner involvement has led to some colleges being formal partners in programmes with staff secondments. Staff undertaking higher degrees may participate in research networks. However, there is little evidence that being research-active is systematically encouraged, recorded or rewarded across HE in FE provision – but the new strand of the TQEF will provide some resource (directly or indirectly) to support research-informed teaching.

Considerations:

- How will ITT requirements for the FE and HE sectors be addressed?
- How are contractual issues addressed, particularly where staff work on both HE and FE programmes?

- Are staff undergoing continuous professional development to address their responsibilities with regard to quality assurance and level and content of the curriculum?
- Is HEFCE funding (direct or indirect) utilised to support the enhancement of learning and teaching?
- Is scholarly activity promoted and recognised?

The higher education environment

Student identity

Students perceive themselves as studying in higher education for different reasons and in different contexts. This can be more marked for those HE students who have progressed internally within the college and react well to somewhat different circumstances. The sense of identity as an HE student can be achieved by the physical environment but also by the range of activities summarised below.

Table 7.3 Developing student identity

Student representatives	A mechanism that enables students to represent the views of their peers on programme committees (which is a requirement of many validations) or in a separate HE group allows input directly into the progress and review of the programme. This will gain importance in IQER. Some colleges train their HE representatives, occasionally with the help of the National Union of Students' training programme, through the local HEI Student Union.
Mentors	Some colleges arrange mentor support for their HE students. This could be a student on a higher level mentoring a first year or, especially in vocational programmes, an industrial mentor. This kind of support is especially helpful for part-time students, who can feel isolated while studying.
Rights and responsibilities	In the supportive environment of a college, it is important that HE students understand that they have both rights and responsibilities. Some requirements will be more rigorous than they may be used to, for example, deadlines for completing assignments.
Graduation	Marking the achievement of graduation is an important celebratory occasion for all higher education students. Those students on franchised HE programmes and many on programmes validated by an HEI will take part in the university's graduation ceremony. This does not usually apply to part-time students, so some colleges have effective graduation ceremonies of their own for their HE students and their family and friends.

The physical environment

For some time there has been a debate about whether higher education should be delivered in colleges with dedicated resources and even in a separate centre or whether it is more appropriate to integrate higher and further education within the college. The stance taken by any one college can follow along a continuum which has at one end a philosophical position, rooted in a strong belief in inclusivity, diversity and equal opportunities and, at the other, a pragmatic decision based on the size of the provision, the location of college buildings, the specialist facilities available and any potential for capital funding. We explore the arguments for both below.

Table 7.4 Integration or separation?

Considerations	Integrated FE and HE	HE centre
HE students like to feel different from FE students (especially young ones) and to be treated differently	This is true in most cases but has as a corollary the fact that younger students usually respond well and behave better when there are more mature students around.	A separate centre offers an opportunity for a more exclusive learning experience.
HE students believe they gain from having access to spaces that are specific to them – library, common room and social facilities	Learning resource centres in colleges can be noisy places (frequently used as a social space). A quiet room, possibly with extended opening hours, can be of real help.	The LSC space ratios do not usually allow for social space, even in a separate centre. In an exclusively HE environment, the refectory and common spaces may feel more comfortable. On the other hand, if the library is separate, it may not house sufficient book stock, journals or periodicals.
HE students commonly have assessments that require working in groups and group presentations and need dedicated facilities	It can be difficult to find a space for small group work, although colleges do operate booking systems for small tutorial rooms or empty classrooms.	This will only be different if the HE centre is not as busy as the rest of the college.
HE students frequently benefit from access to the resources of a local HEI	College libraries frequently offer induction to their own libraries and accompany new entrants to the HEI library. Inter-library loan systems operate well and many HEIs also lend books through college libraries. Access to student union or sports facilities is also negotiated in some cases.	

Table 7.4 Integration or separation? (continued)

Considerations	Integrated FE and HE	HE centre
HE students may feel that they need specific access to IT	Large drop-in centres, whether they operate booking systems or not, can be a problem for HE students looking for a quiet environment and with deadlines to meet. Longer opening hours help HE students who are more likely to start early or work later in the day.	Dedicated IT facilities are usually available and may offer more stable access in a quieter environment.
HE students in vocational areas might also need to access specialist facilities, e.g. in design or engineering, in their own time	Since the introduction of CoVEs with some impressive facilities and resources, sharing these between HE and FE students is an advantage to all. In specialist areas, the fact that state of the art facilities are available and cannot be replicated becomes one of the strongest arguments for integrating HE and FE students.	A separate HE centre which cannot provide the specialist facilities its students require will probably not work well, especially if students have to move around the college to gain such access. This will make a difference according to the curriculum offered.
	Gaining sufficient access to high-quality resources can be managed successfully by careful timetabling: for example, if FE students attend college for one half of the week and HE students for the other, they both have appropriate access to resources and can hold down part-time jobs in the non-timetabled part of the week.	
Because of their commitments, mature HE students need to be able to work from home	There are mature students in both FE and HE (especially Access students bridging the FE and HE progression gap) and they are all likely to have such needs. A well-structured, accessible virtual learning environment (VLE) will make it possible for students with IT equipment at home to access a range of online materials and learning resources.	

Table 7.4 Integration or separation? (continued)

Considerations	Integrated FE and HE	HE centre
HE students usually have to earn while they learn	Most students have to earn and learn, so judicious timetabling that takes this into account will help.	This may be more of a problem after variable tuition fees have been introduced in 2006, especially for part-time students who pay fees up-front and have less financial support available to them.
Staff who teach HE only prefer an HE environment	The discussions between FE and HE staff (and staff teaching both) can enrich the teaching and learning of students in both sectors	Staff may feel more able to undertake scholarly activities in a dedicated HE environment. It is also easier for them to focus on the HE aspects of the college rather than everything required in the learning and skills sector.

Considerations:

- Are there structures and mechanisms in place to give students a learning experience equivalent to that they would receive in an HEI?
- Are students encouraged to give their views and represent their peers?
- Should resources for FE and for HE students be shared or separate?
- Is sufficient account taken of the lives students lead, without absolving them of responsibility?
- Are there arrangements for students to access appropriate resources in terms of library, IT and specialist equipment?

8 Issues and questions

In this final section, we bring together themes that emerge from our understanding of the changing context for higher and further education and the demands of managing the college contribution to higher-level work. We pose a number of questions about the present and future role of colleges in English higher education. We do not attempt to second-guess the direction of public policy, but our concluding discussion is based on three assumptions.

First, we expect to see higher education continue as part of the mission and work of many colleges. Whether this is styled 'higher level skills' or 'higher education' or both is another matter. Second, the two-sector system in England is likely to remain the dominant framework for policy, funding and quality assurance, at least for the time being. Finally, competition and collaboration between institutions in each sector will accompany the next phase of expansion as it did the shift to mass higher education, albeit now under more uncertain conditions.

In the years since the Dearing inquiry made its recommendations on higher education in further education in 1997, the role of colleges in the delivery of higher-level education and skills has been endorsed by each of the Blair governments that followed. In the first administration, responsibility for the funding and quality assurance of all undergraduate and postgraduate education passed to HEFCE and the QAA. This reduced the size, but not necessarily the significance, of the non-prescribed provision funded by the FEFC (and, subsequently, the LSC). With this larger remit came an increase in the policy and guidance addressed to higher education in the college sector.

During the second Blair government, this level of attention increased again, through colleges taking a key role in the delivery of Foundation degrees and, in most cases, being funded indirectly rather than directly for this activity. The third administration re-emphasised the importance of the college contribution to vocational and employer-focused higher education, especially its accessibility, flexibility and capacity to widen participation. In its 2006–07 grant letter, the government asked HEFCE to pursue two major priorities, not just in the short run but 'in developing strategy for the longer term'. The first urged further work on widening participation and the second involved a strategy of growth through employer-led and skills-focused higher education.

The latter is intended to lead to 'radical changes' in the provision of higher education in England, by means of incentives that promote programmes partly or wholly designed, funded or provided by employers. This might include opportunities for:

part-time study and short-cycle courses; a curriculum that changes more quickly in response to learner and employer demand; a more diverse range of providers, including reinforcement of the role of FE colleges in delivering HE; and new private provision.

(DfES, DTI, DNP and HM Treasury 2005: 2)

Similarly, in the HEFCE strategic plan for 2006–11, it is expected that the delivery of higher education in colleges, in the workplace and at home, will increase. To help this happen, there will be a streamlining of the arrangements for funding, monitoring and quality assurance. In terms of employer engagement, this could mean a 'more active role' for colleges in providing courses and services to business that 'address local and regional needs'. In relation to widening participation, however, there were some key strategic risks, especially if there is insufficient demand for higher education places and no increase in the rate of progression for those with vocational qualifications.

In relation to weak demand and an insufficient increase in representation from the under-represented socio-economic groups, this could be due to:

higher fees deterring debt-averse students; poor information, advice and guidance; widening participation being marginalised in some universities and colleges; insufficient growth; and/or those universities and colleges most likely to widen participation struggling in the new market conditions.

(HEFCE 2005: 17)

In relation to no increase in the rate of vocational progression, this could be due to:

a failure of Lifelong Learning Networks to recruit students, or to agree or operate progression agreements that guarantee progression for learners on vocational programmes; a failure in other collaborations between HEIs and FECs; or a failure of HEIs and/or FECs to make vocational opportunities available over a lifetime. (ibid.)

In the parallel grant letter sent to the LSC (as to HEFCE), the priorities set out for colleges are addressed to improving the achievement and participation of young people and, for adults, securing much higher achievement of basic skills and 'the platform of skills for employability at level 2, with stronger progression to level 3 and beyond'. To meet national priorities:

we need to shift the pattern so we provide longer and more expensive courses for adults, to equip them with the range of skills they need for employability and further progression to higher levels of training. As a consequence, the number of publicly funded places on shorter courses which do not lead to national qualifications is likely to fall.

(DfES, DTI, DWP and HM Treasury 2005: 2)

Although aware of concerns about the need to protect return-to-study provision and opportunities for progression through to level 3, colleges were expected to offset the reduction in funding for short courses by offering a wider range of programmes at full cost.

In each of these statements are issues and questions that bear on the management of higher education in colleges through to the end of the decade and beyond. On the one side are features of policy and policy-making that we have highlighted throughout the book. On the other are renewed commitments and risk assessments that will, we believe, benefit colleges that take a strategic view of their involvement in higher education. By way of conclusion, three areas of strategic choice and judgement are briefly explored.

Sustainability and agility?

Unless central to the strategy and management of the college, a decision to begin or continue to provide higher education is less likely to be planned and supported to achieve sustainability in the long term. At one level, this is about building an infrastructure and intelligence to assess the viability of programmes as well as meet the operational requirements and quality standards for their effective delivery. As we have shown, these requirements are extensive. Most are externally driven, centrally or through partner HEIs, and they are subject to regular modification and, sometimes, abrupt change. Even if the provision is small, the demands on management and coordination are no less important, especially if combinations of direct and indirect funding are involved.

At another level, one shared with other parts of the college curriculum, the management task is to demonstrate responsiveness and, at the same time, provide conditions in which higher level work can develop in coherent, controlled and sustainable ways. A more competitive environment for recruiting undergraduate students and, in some regions and localities, a more active market in validation, franchising and other services, will impact directly on the sustainability of higher education in further education settings.

Since they do not award their own higher education qualifications, colleges depend on external organisations for this function. Those directly funded for their higher-level work can choose between the brands, fees and services offered by rival awarding, validating and examining bodies. Those indirectly funded for their higher education will choose, where they can, between the collaborative and financial arrangements offered by degree-awarding institutions. Against the benefits of a strategic and more stable partnership with a single HEI must be weighed the opportunities of collaborating with different and changing sets of degree-awarding establishments.

More difficult to predict is the influence of a new generation of short-cycle higher education programmes, led by the Foundation degree, whose design and course life is linked to the changing skills base in particular occupational sectors. Such courses represent specific and rapid responses to existing skills shortages or emerging skills needs. Sustainability in this context will demand an infrastructure for higher-level work that can support the rise, retreat and renewal of short-order and short-life qualifications. Whether colleges or universities are best placed to handle these demands is less a question than which institutions in each sector have a strategy to build this capability.

In the post-Dearing era, governments have not sought to differentiate higher education by where it is delivered, nor by what sort of institution should provide higher-level work. For college providers of higher education, as for higher education elsewhere, an essentially market-based approach is evident. In respect of general further education colleges, there are strong policy pressures to adopt vocational missions and specialisms, but no attempt to identify which among them should or should not teach courses of higher education. The policy assumption is that higher education provision of good quality is compatible with the vocational mission of a high-performing college. Where a college is judged to be offering poor vocational provision, the view is that improvement of this provision should take precedence over the pursuit of higher education.

Following the 2006 White Paper on further education, some of these assumptions are set to change. The view now taken is that not all colleges are well placed to provide higher education. Similarly, where higher-level work is not delivered to the appropriate standard, colleges should not continue with this provision. In the same document, HEFCE is asked to review the effectiveness of small pockets of higher education in further education and, with the LSC, to review the financial arrangements (direct and indirect) that underpin higher education courses in colleges.

Integration and ownership?

The diverse provision, distribution and development of higher education in individual colleges has given rise to widely different levels and types of management. One of the arguments running through the book is the importance of a strategic approach to the management and coordination of higher education, no matter what size the provision. Sustainability is one strategic concern. Another is integration.

By 'integration' we mean the linkage of higher education to the larger activity, overall management and core mission of the college. It will apply to the single course of higher education taught by a college as much as to the mix of programmes offered by a major provider of undergraduate and postgraduate education. Integration might encompass other types of higher education or other levels of provision in the same college. Equally, it might extend to provision in other institutions, through collaborative partnerships and networks of further, higher and adult education providers.

The opportunities made available to students for internal progression, between levels 4 and 5 as well as between 3 and 4, flow from the work accomplished on course and curriculum integration. Articulation and progression agreements between a college and its partner HEIs, but also with other colleges, will add to these opportunities through both outward and inward transfer. For the college, the cultivation and coordination of these pathways, including their monitoring, cannot but be a major aspect of the management of higher education.

A neglected issue in the effort to reform and rebuild vocational higher education is the presence in some colleges of undergraduate programmes in academic subjects in the arts, humanities and social sciences. Frequently, these are found where colleges are filling a geographical gap in the provision of higher education. Although offered mainly at the honours level, there is no reason in principle why short-cycle versions of general higher education, suitably chosen, should not find a place in further education. As with other higher level work in further education, such programmes might be taught in colleges but belong to a curriculum and credit framework whose development is the responsibility of a local or regional network of institutions.

That curriculum integration, planning and management might operate beyond the college is in accord with the idea of 'managed provider networks', as advanced in the Foster report (Foster 2005). Already found in other public sector services, networked provider systems are a means of managing activity collectively as well as independently, rationalising administrative services and use of buildings, and sponsoring shared service arrangements, 'either hosted by one member of the confederation or supplied by an agency'.

The provision of higher education in further education is an obvious candidate for models of this kind but, equally, there are good reasons why a number of colleges have sought to create a discrete structure and identity for this activity within their institutions. In these examples, curriculum integration is accompanied by organisational and spatial separation, as in higher education centres or faculties and designated campuses or buildings.

Generally, the rationale for separation is some combination of three dimensions. One is administrative and driven by the need to deal efficiently and effectively with organisations that fund, review and share in the delivery of higher education programmes. Another is associative and aimed at recognising an undergraduate or higher education identity for students (and some staff). A third is to do with ethos and environment: the need to foster, realise and demonstrate a culture of higher learning.

Just how much detachment is expressed in these arrangements will, of course, vary. Most higher education students will share some facilities with the rest of the college, and some of these same students will access teaching and resources provided by a partner HEI. Some staff will do all their work at the higher education levels. Others will have further education as the larger or smaller part of their teaching. The conditions of service for staff in colleges, including the amount of class contact, continue to set them apart from their colleagues in HEIs. Nevertheless, there is evidence of convergence in some areas, especially where teaching-only contracts are deployed in HEIs and where opportunities for scholarship and research are available to college lecturers.

Boundary marking will also say something about the strategic profile of higher education in the college and, commonly if more tacitly, how much control and ownership is claimed by the college for the higher-level work that is undertaken. A college strategy for higher education can give confidence to directions and decisions that take a wider and longer view of further education than that addressed to the here and now. An argument for (or against) an involvement in higher education is for each college to make on the basis of its own assessment of opportunities, costs and risks.

In an earlier era, a growing maturity in providing good-quality higher education was, for some mixed economy institutions, acknowledged in devolved arrangements for quality assurance, including partnership in validation. As envisaged in the Foster review, the further education system of the future would see colleges, 'led by the best', moving towards self-regulation and away from invasive centralism. Over time, we also expect colleges to exercise more responsibility for the quality of the higher education they provide, even though some arrangements such as franchising might serve to delay this process. More than that, we see the goal of self-regulation benefiting in a broader way from the critical self-assessment and independence expected of higher education.

Small and strategic?

Lastly, we return to the situation in which most colleges find themselves: that of small or medium-size providers of higher education in institutions predominantly concerned with further education. Why provision that is modest in size should be managed seriously and strategically is the chief justification for this book. This is not to privilege higher education in the work of colleges, although its perceived status has been a magnet for some lecturers and, at times, a source of tension. Nor do we assume that all colleges should engage in higher-level work or that the delivery of more higher education will improve the overall quality of education in colleges. Both are interesting questions, but neither has been publicly debated or systematically researched.

Our contention is simply that, given a two-sector system and policies to expand higher education in further education, the management of this activity will involve systems, organisations, relationships and assumptions different from those normally operated in the learning and skills sector. In any one college, a variety of funding, quality and reporting arrangements might apply, even where there are just a few programmes. These too will be subject to change, sometimes rapid and far-reaching. As courses of higher education, they often acquire more visibility than other programmes in the college, especially when their quality and standards are reviewed by the QAA. When delivering a flagship qualification, such as the Foundation degree, the profile of the provision is higher again, although the risks are shared with other partners.

Compared to the mass environments of most universities, further education colleges typically recruit smaller numbers to their higher education programmes and teach them in smaller classes. Not only has this scale of activity enabled them to adopt a more supportive and intensive style of teaching than in many HEIs, it has served as the main claim for the distinctiveness of higher education in college settings. Alongside the vocational orientation of their higher education, and its accessibility to local and non-traditional students, the intimacy and student-centred pedagogy of further education have been reasons for the government to view colleges as major sites for building progression and broadening participation in undergraduate education. For this policy purpose, at least, the smaller courses and cohorts in further education are a major advantage.

Where the responsibility is to distribute public funding for higher education, a similar regard for the student experience led HEFCE to sponsor college provision that was sufficient in size and linkage to sustain the 'quality, standards and culture' properly associated with higher education. According to the council, where there is a small volume of higher education in a college whose focus and mission is oriented towards further education, it can be harder to safeguard the quality of the student experience. There is a danger that such provision may become 'isolated' because it is neither securely rooted in the core further education work of the college nor linked through partnerships to the wider higher education community.

Again, when allocating development funds to colleges, the aim is to encourage a 'critical mass'. Eligibility for these funds is therefore restricted to colleges with amounts of higher education 'more than marginal to the institutional mission' and which wished to offer significant higher education provision 'on a long-term basis'. Notwithstanding these efforts, and the legal controls on what can be supported as higher education in colleges, the other way that small pockets of prescribed higher education receive funding is through franchising, especially where only part of a programme is taught in further education.

Given the diversity of English higher education, notably the variety of modes of study, there is an understandable reluctance to issue specific guidance on the volume or threshold of higher education in any particular setting. Similarly, little or no attempt is made by the sector bodies to elaborate on the 'higherness' of higher education, except in terms of qualification levels, qualification descriptors and subject benchmarks. For its part, the QAA has commented only occasionally on such matters, and almost always in subject review reports on individual colleges.

All the same, there are legitimate reasons why scale and its implications for the quality and challenge of higher education should be a regular concern in the management of colleges. Even for large and established providers, there are questions to ask about the relationship of new and existing programmes to centres of academic and vocational expertise, both internal and external. What is understood by critical mass, and how it is best achieved or improved, should be established as a strategic imperative.

Yet, this is to assume that higher education is routinely represented in college thinking and planning. Often this is not the case. The volume and variety of higher-level work is usually encountered in its parts and only exceptionally considered or conceived as a whole. At a time when the college contribution to higher education is the object of more policy and more guidance, the flow of information and intelligence is not easily shared or collectively owned. In assembling this text, we too have been struck by the disparate ways that colleges acquire their understanding of the requirements of higher education.

Appendix A
Selected terminology

A selection of key terms is examined below because they have ambiguous or contested meanings, have changed their meaning, or have multiple meanings.

In Part One (Chapter 2), this has been addressed in our contextualisation of FE in HE. In Part Two, we have used the terms in reporting on: organisation (Chapter 3), funding (Chapter 4), partnerships (Chapter 5), quality (Chapter 6) and curriculum (Chapter 7) and have used the terms in context.

For each term, we give our definition and application of the term with, where appropriate, the range of usage.

Higher education (HE) sector

The publicly funded HE sector (in England) comprises the higher education institutions (HEIs) funded by HEFCE (set up under the Further and Higher Education Act 1992, which combined the remit of the Universities Funding Council (UFC) and the Polytechnics and Colleges Funding Council (PCFC)). HEIs include those institutions granted university title ('universities') and those specialist and general colleges designated as higher education colleges (some of which may include the term 'university college' in their title). Not all higher education colleges have degree-awarding powers. Degree-awarding powers and university title can be awarded by the Privy Council and the number of universities and other colleges in the sector has changed year-on-year (see page 41).

Further education (FE) sector

The Further and Higher Education Act of 1992 set up the FEFC and identified courses fundable in the FE sector in schedule 2. Under the 1992 Act, further education colleges were able to transfer to the HE sector if their FTEs for HE were 55 per cent or more of their total enrolment.

The Learning and Skills Act of 2000 replaced the FEFC with the LSC and broadened the sector to include other providers and a planning as well as a funding remit.

Prescribed higher education

'Prescribed' higher education is that provision defined under the relevant Education Acts and Statutory Instruments, and this and the default term 'non-prescribed' higher education determines if it is within the remit of the Higher Education Funding Council or of the Learning and Skills Council.

The 1988 Education Reform Act removed the 'duty' to secure provision for higher education in their area from the remit of local education authorities (LEAs) and set up the PCFC (alongside the UFC). LEAs, however, retained the 'power' to secure provision (with regard for facilities provided by HEIs).

Schedule 6 of the Act listed the 'courses of higher education' which constituted higher education provision. This included courses for the further training of teachers and youth and community workers, postgraduate, first degree, Diploma of Higher Education, Higher National Diploma or Higher National Certificate of the Business & Technician Education Council, Diploma in Management Studies, and the Certificate of Education, along with courses in preparation for a professional examination at a higher level and courses providing education at a higher level. 'Higher level' was defined as above advanced GCE or BTEC National.

However, the Education (Prescribed Courses of Higher Education) Regulations in 1989 excluded some of this provision. Excluded from postgraduate courses were those preparing solely for a professional examination at a higher level, and only full-time and sandwich DipHEs and HNDs were included. Full-time and sandwich courses of more than a year's duration providing education at a higher level not defined as postgraduate or first degree were however included if they prepared for an award of the Council for National Academic Awards (CNAA).

In 1993, the schedule of prescribed courses was broadened for Wales – The Education (Prescribed Courses of Higher Education) (Wales) Regulations 1993 – and in 1998 this definition was applied to England. BTEC HNCs were added to the schedule along with part-time courses of at least two years' duration leading to awards from institutions granted awarding powers by the Privy Council.

Non-prescribed higher education (NPHE)

Non-prescribed higher education is therefore those qualifications not included in the regulations as prescribed. These qualifications remained within the remit of the LEAs and subsequently the FEFC and LSC.

After the recommendations of the Dearing committee in 1997 (see page 8) some NPHE was defined as prescribed (see above) and funding responsibility for all prescribed HE (that residually funded by FEFC and the newly defined prescribed HE, largely HNCs) was transferred to HEFCE.

Nonetheless, there remains a significant amount of NPHE provision in colleges funded by the LSC. Under the Learning and Skills Act 2000, the LSC has the power to fund courses falling within schedule 6 of the 1988 Act, paragraphs (g) and (h), which related generically to courses at higher levels preparing for professional examinations and other higher-level provision, that is provision which was not included as prescribed in the subsequent Regulations. While much NPHE was categorised as 'Other' by the LSC (i.e. provision which did not lead to a qualification as approved by the Secretary of State and included in Sections 96 and 97 of the 2000 Act), it was fundable. NPHE courses are among those being approved on to the NQF at its higher levels (see below).

Higher education/higher-level

'Higher-level' was defined in the 1988 Act (see above) as those courses above what has since been described in the NQF as level 3 qualifications.

'HE in FE' is defined by the level of the qualification aim. It is governed, in England, by the two qualifications frameworks of the Qualifications Curriculum Authority (QCA) and the Quality Assurance Agency (QAA) respectively. Usage of the term may, or may not (see Chapter 2), include both prescribed and non-prescribed higher education.

The national qualifications framework (NQF) covering England, Wales and Northern Ireland, which came into effect on 1 September

2004 (replacing that of 2000), sets out the levels at which individual qualifications can be recognised by the regulatory authorities. Under these regulations, there are nine levels: entry level to level 8.

Entry to level 3 was unchanged from 2004, but the 'higher' levels of 4 and 5 were revised to levels 4 to 8. This allowed for clearer links with the framework for higher education qualifications in England, Wales and Northern Ireland (FHEQ) published by the QAA in 2001.

The QCA framework allows qualifications to be positioned but does not indicate that they have the same purpose, content or outcomes; nonetheless, it is supported by level descriptors or 'indicators' representing common standards. The NQF revisions supported the new framework for achievement (FfA) which is underpinned by a unit and credit-based system (see below).

The QAA framework (part of the QAA Academic Infrastructure) places the (generic) HE qualifications awarded by universities and higher education colleges at each of five levels. It describes (or benchmarks) the qualification in terms of its particular purpose and general characteristics and provides qualification descriptors exemplifying the outcomes of the main qualification at each level and the nature of the change between levels. (Additionally, the QAA has a specific Foundation Degree Qualification Benchmark (FDQB) and a series of subject benchmark statements for honours degrees.)

These five levels are numbered 1 to 5 (with 1, 2, 3 roughly corresponding to the years of study to obtain a full-time honours degree). The alphabetic descriptors correspond to the level of the final award but, in practice, each level represents bands of qualifications sharing similar outcomes.

In summary:

Table A.1

National Qualifications Framework		Framework for Higher Education Qualifications (2001)	
Original levels (2000)	Revised levels (2004)		
5	8	D (doctoral)	5
	7	M (masters)	4
4	6	H (honours)	3
	5	I (intermediate)	2
	4	C (certificates)	1

Clearly there is potential for confusion if the numberings in the QAA system are used for comparison with the QCA (and the frameworks for Wales, Northern Ireland and Scotland, and Europe). However, the systems are aligned and there is a commonality, with (credit-based) frameworks running from entry through 1 to 8 and the use of levels 4 to 8 (instead of 1 to 5) becoming more commonplace.

In the book we have, therefore, adopted the convention of using the NQF numerical levels for non-prescribed higher education (4–7), and intermediate (including HNC/Ds, Foundation degrees), honours and masters for prescribed.

For England, details can be obtained from the QCA website: www.qca.org.uk, and from the QAA: www.qaa.ac.uk.

Credit frameworks

The concept of 'earning credit' may simply mean accumulating numerically accredited modules toward a defined total for a qualification. However, 'credit frameworks' as referenced in this book allocate a credit volume to units at levels, and the award of a qualification is made against specified rules of combination.

There has been a range of initiatives related to unitised and credit-based frameworks both within and across further and higher education for many years. Many HEIs have developed internal credit frameworks, some with partner colleges. At a national level, the Open College Networks in England, Wales and Northern Ireland provide credit-based awards. There are cross-sector agreements with regard to credit in Wales and Northern Ireland and Scotland.

Over time there has been a move to consensus on a framework of levels (albeit with different descriptors) ranging from entry through levels 1 to 8. The NQF uses these levels for its qualifications framework (this allocates qualifications to levels, not elements of qualifications) and this is aligned to the credit and qualifications framework being developed which is unit-based and supported by a system of credit accumulation and transfer.

The review of the HEFCE Teaching Funding Methodology includes a commitment to consider methods of funding by credit.

Franchise and consortium

The terms franchise and consortium are used in two ways within the text: one with regard to 'indirect' funding arrangements as defined by HEFCE (see in particular Chapters 3 and 4) and a second with regard to arrangements for delivery of validated programmes (see in particular Chapter 6).

'Direct' funding is funding provided by HEFCE directly to a provider of higher education. All HEIs are directly funded and approximately half of college providers receive direct funding. 'Indirect' funding is chanelled via another institution, either by a 'franchise' or a 'consortium' relationship. Commonly colleges receive more than one form of funding (see Chapter 3, page 40 and Chapter 4, page 58). For indirectly funded partnerships, guidance is provided in the HEFCE codes of practice, 00/54.

Franchise: with regard to funding, franchise applies to virtually all collaborative funding arrangements, including many that colleges may refer to as consortia, such as for the delivery of Foundation degrees. Where a student is registered at one institution but taught at another, this is described as a franchise. The funding flows from HEFCE to the franchising institution and the proportion passed on is at the discretion of the franchising institution. Commonly HEIs franchise out to colleges, although there is a small amount of franchising from one college to another. HEFCE publishes annual data on the number of wholly and partially franchised students (two years in arrears until 2006). HEFCE counsel that the data should be treated with caution because of the diversity of franchise agreements and the different interpretations of the guidance on completing the (HESA) data returns. However, in 2004–05 there were 51,018 students, comprising 35,389 FTEs, recorded as franchised to further education colleges in England (see page 59).

With regard to collaboration over curriculum development and delivery, franchise is commonly used to describe an arrangement whereby an HEI 'franchises' a college to deliver a programme owned by the HEI under agreed terms and within the quality assurance regime of the HEI. The franchising institution normally retains overall control of the programme's content, delivery, assessment and quality assurance arrangements. This arrangement may be directly or indirectly funded (see page 110).

Consortium: with regard to funding, this term applies only to 'HEFCE-recognised funding consortia'; it is a mechanism for distributing grant to a group of institutions through a single lead institution. In 2005–06 there were nine consortia, three of which were led by colleges. Here the funding from HEFCE passes to the lead institution but the students are registered at the partner delivering the programme. However, it may be that the consortium uses a term such as 'partnership' to title its arrangements (see page 59).

With regard to collaborative arrangements for curriculum development and delivery, a partnership of higher and further education institutions may describe itself as a 'consortium' without being an HEFCE-recognised funding consortium. Such arrangements are common for subject-based collaborations, including Foundation degrees (see page 110).

Collaborative provision

Again this term is commonly used in two contexts: funding and curriculum.

In relation to funding, the term is used by HEFCE to collectively describe both forms of indirect funding, that is franchise and consortium (see above). There are HEFCE codes of practice relating to both forms.

In relation to curriculum provision, the term is used by QAA to describe provision leading to an award by an awarding HEI which is delivered and/or supported and/or assessed through an arrangement with a partner organisation. This is covered by section 2 of the QAA code of practice.

Appendix B
Key funding initiatives
and documents

Legislation, policy and funding documents	Summary	Commentary
Evaluation of the Funding Method of Teaching, November 1995 (CP 2/95)	Consultation on the characteristics, principles and elements of a new funding method for teaching.	New model introduced for 1998–99 after delay to take account of findings of Dearing Inquiry.
Higher Education in Further Education Colleges: Funding the Relationship, 1995 (M 1/95)	To stimulate discussion on the future of the FE/HE interface, the role of FE colleges in providing higher education and the funding arrangements for HE work in FE colleges.	Noted that the Average Units of Council Funding (AUCF) for HE in FE was significantly lower than in HEIs.
Higher Education in Further Education Colleges: A Future Funding Approach, 1996 (M 3/96)	Recognised the increasing diversity of provision funding arrangements.	Proposed that consideration should be given in the medium to long term to restructuring the organisation of HE funding in FECs through a framework based on collaboration or consortia arrangements.
Study of the Relative Costs of HE Provision in FE Colleges and HE Institutions, 1998 (98/57)	Report of research commissioned to investigate relative costs.	Found significant variations across the matched sample within and between sectors. FECs provided more small-class teaching and personal tutoring but the academic staffing costs were similar because the cost of the academic staff was lower in FECs.
The Nature of Higher and Further Education Sub-contractual Partnerships, 1998, (98/58)	Report of research commissioned to examine the financial, administrative and quality aspects of sub-contractual partnerships.	Found that (under the old funding model) the amount paid to FECs varied from £990 to £2,200 for band 1 students and from £1,600 to £4,143 for band 2.

Legislation, policy and funding documents	Summary	Commentary
Funding Method for Teaching from 1998–99, 1996 (21/96)	Established a standard price for FTEs in each of four price groups with a premium weighting for certain categories of student and institution. There was to be migration toward a formula-based calculation of standard resource. Additional student numbers would be subject to bidding.	The method was set out in *Funding Higher Education in England: How the HEFCE allocates its funds* (98/67), and annually thereafter.
Higher Education in the Learning Society, 1997	Dearing inquiry reports. From 1999 HEFCE became responsible for funding all first degree, postgraduate, HND and C Dip HE and Cert Ed provision delivered by FECs. However, non-prescribed HE remained fundable by the FEFC.	Number of recommendations about HE in FE, including that FECs should focus on sub-degree provision (and that such provision should be the main area of expansion of HE); that all HE in FECs should be funded by HEFCE; and that, where possible, funding should be received directly rather than indirectly.
Funding Higher Education in Further Education Colleges, 1998 (98/59)	Consultation in the light of transfer of funding for prescribed HE from FEFC to HEFCE for 1999–2000 and proposed new arrangements for 2000–01.	Referred to the findings of the commissioned reports on costs and sub-contractual relationships.
Higher Education in Further Education Colleges: Guidance for colleges on funding options, 1999 (99/36)	Set out the options for future funding for colleges.	Colleges asked to identify their choice of direct funding, franchising or funding through a consortia. Multiple routes possible but single encouraged.
Higher Education in Further Education Colleges. Indirectly Funded Partnerships: codes of practice for franchise and consortia arrangements, 2000 (00/54)	Combined Code of Practice bringing together separate codes after consultation. Sets out the principles which partnerships should reflect.	Indicated that partnerships would be surveyed in the future.
Review of Indirect Funding Agreements and Arrangements Between Higher Education Institutions and Further Education Colleges, 2000 (2003/57)	Report of commissioned review of operation of indirect funding agreements.	Reported significant variation persisting, with HEIs reporting retention of funding of from 2.75% to 42% while FECs reported from 8% to 50%.

Legislation, policy and funding documents	Summary	Commentary
The Future of Higher Education, 2003	HE White Paper.	Expressed the intention to continue to increase participation toward the 50% target, mainly through two-year, work-focused, Foundation degrees, often delivered in FE colleges. In order to maintain quality, structured HE/FE partnerships (franchise or consortia funding arrangements) to be the primary vehicles. Direct funding to be considered on a case-by-case basis by HEFCE. Proposed variable fees.
Higher Education Act 2004	Implemented variable fees.	Offa established to approve access agreements required when fees above standard charged from 2006–07.
Review of the Teaching Funding Method, 2005 (2005/41)	Consultation on changes to the method.	
Review of the Teaching Funding Method. Outcomes of First Cycle of Consultation, 2006 (2006/12)		Set out the decisions made by HEFCE following responses to the consultation and summarised the responses received.
Improving the Student Financial Service. Report of the Review of HE Student Finance Delivery in England, 2006	DfES report setting out recommendations and options to improve the administration of student finance.	Government responded by announcing the reform of the Student Loans Company (SLC) to become the customer-focused national delivery organisation for the service to be operational for September 2008 applications for 2009–10 entry.
Further Eductaion: Rising Skills, Improving Life Chances, 2006	FE White Paper	Proposed to develop colleges; role in HE in regions where access to HE institutions is limited, working through LLNs. Prioritiesed the economic mission, a focus on employability, and links with employers to provide work-based HE programmes through HE centres of excellence. Capital support to be explored.

Appendix C
Guide to organisations and resources

Organisation	Summary	Publications	Accessing the organisation
Adult Learning Inspectorate (ALI)	The part of the further education inspection system that dealt with adult provision. Merged into Ofsted in 2006.		www.ali.gov.uk
Association of Colleges (AoC)	The representative organisation for further education. Has an HE in FE group that discusses policy and practice and an annual HE in FE conference, jointly delivered with HEFCE from 2006.	A range of publications; monthly Curriculum and Quality briefing.	www.aoc.co.uk
Association of Collaborative Providers (ACP)	A group of HEIs and consortia that meets to discuss collaborative arrangements. A combination of what was formerly the HEFCE Major Franchisers Group and CoCo (the Consortium of Consortia).		Contact: Chris Green: c.green@onetel.net

Organisation	Summary	Publications	Accessing the organisation
Council of Validating Universities	An organisation with HE and FE membership to promote and share good practice in collaborative provision. Has an annual conference.	A range of publications including a handbook on quality assurance.	www.cvu.ac.uk
Department for Education and Skills (DfES)	The DfES leads on the implementation of government policy in all aspects of education and skills. It has a portal (www.direct.gov.uk) which includes information and advice on higher education, including on student finance. Predecessor departments were the Department for Education and Science (DES) and the Department for Education and Employment (DfEE).	*The Future of Higher Education*, White Paper, 2003 *Foundation Degree Task Force Report to Ministers*, 2004 *21st Century Skills*, Skills Strategy White Paper 2003 *Skills: Getting on in business: Getting on at work*, Skills White Paper, 2005 *Realising the Potential*, the Foster review of further education, 2005 'The higher education role of further education colleges', think piece for the Foster Review, Professor Gareth Parry, 2005 *Further Education: Raising Skills, Improving Life Chances*, FE White Paper, 2006 Improving the student Finance Service: Report of the Review of HE Student Finance Delivery in England, 2006	www.dfes.gov.uk www. Foundationdegrees. org.uk www.dfes.gov.uk/ furthereducation/ fereview/evidence. shtml
Edexcel	Incorporates BTEC; the awarding body for higher national qualifications. Colleges can offer programmes off-the-shelf; HEIs can develop programmes under licence.	A range of publications including regular policy briefings. Handbooks for centres and external examiners of HNs.	www.edexcel.org.uk

Organisation	Summary	Publications	Accessing the organisation
The Europe Unit	A sector-wide body working in the interests of UK higher education and addressing European issues.		www.europeunit.ac.uk
Foundation Degree Forward (Fdf)	Announced in the 2003 White Paper, set up in 2004 with a contract then extended until 2008. Remit to promote the development of Fds and disseminate good practice.	In brief: leaflets dealing with APEL, Employer engagement, FE/HE partnership, work-based learning, etc. Journal: *Forward*, quarterly. *National Validation Service Handbook*.	www.fdf.ac.uk Join the JISC email forum by contacting: www.jiscmail.ac.uk/lists/Foundation-Degree-Forum.html
Higher Education Academy (HEA)	Formerly the Learning and Teaching Support Network (LTSN) Generic Centre. Has 24 subject centres and a Senior Adviser for HE in FE; has an annual conference.	Dedicated web pages on HE in *FE Assessment Series*, 2001: eight booklets that deal with such aspects as group assessment, portfolio, work-based learning and plagiarism. *Learning and Employability series*, 2004: six booklets that deal with such aspects as employability and the curriculum, entrepreneurship and widening participation. Has developed the Standards Framework for Teaching and Supporting Student Learning in Higher Education and provides a register of practitioners and an accreditation service for HEIs' training programmes.	www.heacademy.ac.uk

Organisation	Summary	Publications	Accessing the organisation
Higher Education Funding Council for England (HEFCE)	The funding council is responsible for all public funding of prescribed higher education, wherever it takes place. It is not formally a planning body but some of its initiatives affect planning. There is an annual HE in FE conference, jointly delivered with the AoC from 2006. Predecessor funding bodies were the Universities Funding Council (UFC) and the Polytechnics and Colleges Funding Council (PCFC).	*Supporting Higher Education in Colleges: Good practice guide* (03/15), 2003 *Supporting Higher Education in Colleges: Policy and practice* (03/16), 2003 *Information on Quality and Standards in Higher Education: Final guidance* (03/51), 2003 *Review of Indirect Funding Agreements and Arrangements between Higher Education Institutions and Further Education Colleges* (03/57), 2003 *HEFCE Strategic Plan 2003–08* (2005/16), 2005 *HEFCE Strategic Plan 2006–11*, (2006/13), 2006 Lifelong Learning Networks: several circular letters and progress reports, from 2004. Teaching funding review: reports and briefings – use search facility, 2005. Centres of Excellence in Teaching and Learning [05/17]. One of the CETLs at the University of Plymouth (HELP) is specifically for HE in FE. See Appendix B for further funding documents.	www.hefce.ac.uk. This can be used to access all funding guidance and to make statistical returns.

Organisation	Summary	Publications	Accessing the organisation
Joint Information Systems Committee (JISC)	JISC supports further and higher education by providing strategic guidance, advice and opportunities to use Information and Communications Technology (ICT) to support teaching, learning, research and administration. JISC is funded by all the UK post-16 and higher education funding councils.	A range of publications including guides of good practice, see www.jisc.ac.uk/collections	www.jisc.ac.uk
Learning and Skills Council (LSC)	The Further Education Funding Council (FEFC) was replaced in 2001 by the LSC, the funding body for the learning and skills sector which includes FE and non-prescribed HE. The LSC does have a planning function.	*Success for All*, 2003 – government commitment to further education and training *Agenda for Change*, 2005 – fundamental overhaul of complex funding arrangements for FE colleges *Strategy for Higher Education*, 2006	www.lsc.gov.uk
Learning and Skills Network (LSN)	Formerly within the Learning and Skills Development Agency (LSDA). The LSN from 1 April 2006 continued the LSDA research, training and consultancy work. HE in FE research publications were inherited from the predecessor organisation.	Parry, G., and Thompson, A., *Closer by Degrees: The past present and future of higher education in further education colleges*, 2002 Parry, G., Davies, P. and Williams, J., *Dimensions of Difference: Higher education in the learning and skill sector*, 2003 Parry, G., Davies, P. and Williams, J., *Difference, Diversity and Distinctiveness: Higher education in the learning and skills sector*, 2004	www.lsda.org.uk

Organisation	Summary	Publications	Accessing the organisation
Lifelong Learning UK (LLUK)	The Sector Skills Council for education and training. Replaced FENTO (the national training organisation for FE).	The standards for teacher training qualifications for FE in England. These are being replaced by a framework covering teachers, tutors and trainers and leading to qualified status and a licence to practise. This will be implemented in 2007.	www.lifelonglearning. uk.org
Mixed Economy Group (MEG)	MEG represents those further education colleges which have a strategic role in the provision of programmes of higher education. Members have at least 500 FTEs of HE.		Contact: Chair – John Widdowson, Principal of New College Durham: John. Widdowson@newdur. ac.uk
National Institute for Adult and Continuing Education (NIACE)	Funded by the DfES, Niace's remit covers adult and continuing education.	A range of publications that impact on HE in FE.	www.niace.org.uk
Netskills	The quality Internet training service (partly funded by JISC).	Netskills have designed a Professional Development Certificate (PDC) in e-learning. It is accredited by BTEC at level 4 of the NQF.	www.netskills. ac.uk/accreditation

Organisation	Summary	Publications	Accessing the organisation
Office for Standards in Education (Ofsted)	The inspectorate whose responsibility includes inspection of further education colleges, normally covering provision up to level 3 and in some cases, non-prescribed higher education. Previously covered under–19 provision, working with the ALI for over–19 provision. From April 2007 with an expanded remit, it becomes the Office for Standards in Education, Children's Services and Skills.	Reports on colleges on the website – frequently referred to in QAA reviews.	www.ofsted.gov.uk
Quality Assurance Agency for higher education (QAA)	The QAA is responsible for assuring the quality and standards of higher education.	*Report of a Survey – The Provision of the Pilot Programme of Foundation Degrees in Seven Colleges of Further and Higher Education* *Overview report on Foundation Degree reviews, 2003* *Foundation Degree Qualification Benchmark, 2004* *Report of a Survey to Follow up Foundation Degree Reviews Carried Out in 2002–03, 2005* *Learning from Reviews of Foundation Degrees Carried Out in 2004–05, 2006* *Learning from Higher Education in Further Education, 2006*	www.qaa.ac.uk. Includes the documentation related to the Academic Infrastructure and reports on reviews of institutions.
Qualifications Curriculum Authority (QCA)	The QCA is responsible for agreeing the programmes that are included in the National Qualifications Framework (NQF).	*Framework for Achievement, 2005* Building a credit and qualifications framework, June 2006	www.qca.org.uk Includes a comparison of the original and revised levels of the NQF aligned to the FHEQ.

Organisation	Summary	Publications	Accessing the organisation
Quality Improvement Agency for Lifelong Learning (QIA)	Formerly within the Learning and Skills Development Agency (LSDA). The QIA is responsible for quality improvement across the learning and skills sector.	The QIA was operative from 1 April 2006.	www.qia.org.uk
Standing Conference of Principals (SCOP)	The representative organisation of Colleges of Higher Education, a reducing number as more gain university titles.		www.scop.ac.uk
Society for Research in Higher Education (SRHE)	An independent organisation that aims to improve the quality of higher education through the encouragement of debate and publication on issues of policy and on the management of higher education institutions and the curriculum and teaching and learning methods.		www.srhe.ac.uk
Sector Skills Development Agency (SSDA)	Funded by the DfES, the SSDA underpins the skills for business Network made up of the 25 Sector Skills Councils (SSCs).		www.ssda.org.uk
Teaching Quality Information (TQI)	Brings together key sources of official information about the quality of HE in UK universities and colleges.	Information about HE programmes in colleges can be added to the HERO website if colleges wish. Colleges with franchised HE are not currently listed separately from the HEI. However TQI for colleges, and separate listings for franchise provision, are proposed from 2007–08 (HEFCE circular letter 09/2006).	www.tqi.ac.uk

Organisation	Summary	Publications	Accessing the organisation
University for Industry (ufi)	Responsible for the operation of learndirect across England, Wales and Northern Ireland, and UK online centres in England. To support e-learning and e-services. Ufi also runs the free, impartial learndirect advice service.	Operates the Learn through Work platform to enable work-based learning at an individual level.	www.ufi.com
Universities Vocational Awards Council (UVAC)	A not-for-profit organisation with FE and HE membership. Particular interest in workplace learning. Organises an annual conference.	Undertakes research; a range of publications about vocational education.	www.uvac.ac.uk
Universities UK (UUK)	Formerly the Council for Vice Chancellors and Principals (CVCP), UUK is the representative body for universities.		www.universitieuk.ac.uk

References

DfEE (1999) *Learning To Succeed. A new framework for post-16 learning*, Cm 4392, London: The Stationery Office.

DfES (2003a) *The Future of Higher Education*, Cm 5735, London: The Stationery Office.

DfES (2003b) *Success for All. Reforming Further Education and Training*, London: DfES.

DfES (2004) *Foundation Degree Task Force Report to Ministers*, London: DfES.

DfES (2006) *Improving the Student Finance Service. Report of the Review of the Higher Education Student Finance Delivery in England*, London: DfES.

DfES (2006) *Further Education: Raising Skills, Improving Life Chances*, Cm 6768, London: The Stationery Office.

DfES, DTI, DWP and HM Treasury (2003), *21st Century Skills. Realising Our Potential. Individuals, Employers, Nation*, Cm 5810, London: The Stationery Office.

DfES, DTI, DWP and HM Treasury (2005) *Skills: Getting on in business, getting on at work,* Cm 6483, London: The Stationery Office.

Fdf (2006) *Researching foundation degrees. Linking research and practice*, ed. Beaney, P., Litchfield: fdf.

Foster, A. (2005) *Realising the Potential. A review of the future role of further education colleges*, London: DfES.

HEFCE (1995) *Evaluation of the Funding Method for Teaching* (CP 2/95), Bristol: HEFCE.

HEFCE (1995) *Higher Education in Further Education Colleges: Funding the Relationship* (M 1/95), Bristol: HEFCE.

HEFCE (1996) *Funding Method for Teaching from 1998–99* (C 21/96), Bristol: HEFCE.

HEFCE (1996) *Higher Education in Further Education Colleges: A future funding approach* (M 3/96), Bristol: HEFCE.

HEFCE (1998) *Funding Higher Education in Further Education Colleges* (98/59), Bristol: HEFCE.

HEFCE (1998) *Study of the Relative Costs of HE Provision in FE Colleges and HE Institutions* (98/57), Bristol: HEFCE.

HEFCE (1998) *The Nature of Higher and Further Education sub-contractual partnerships* (98/58), Bristol: HEFCE.

HEFCE (1999) *Higher Education in Further Education colleges: Guidance for colleges on funding options* (99/36), Bristol: HEFCE.

HEFCE (2000) *Foundation Degree Prospectus* (00/27), Bristol: HEFCE.

HEFCE (2000), *Higher Education in Further Education Colleges. Indirectly Funded Partnerships: Codes of practice for franchise and consortia arrangements* (00/54), Bristol: HEFCE.

HEFCE (2003a) *Review of Indirect Funding Agreements and Arrangements between Higher Education Institutions and Further Education Colleges* (2003/57), Bristol: HEFCE.

HEFCE (2003b), *Supporting Higher Education in Further Education Colleges. A guide for tutors and lecturers*, (2003/15), Bristol: HEFCE

HEFCE (2003c) *Supporting Higher Education in Further Education Colleges. Policy, practice and prospects* (2003/16), Bristol: HEFCE.

HEFCE (2004) *Lifelong Learning Networks, Joint letter from HEFCE and the Learning and Skills Council*, Circular Letter, 3 June 2004 (12/2004), Bristol: HEFCE.

HEFCE (2005) *Review of the Teaching Funding Method: Consultation on changes to the method* (2005/41), Bristol: HEFCE.

HEFCE (2006) *Review of the Teaching Funding Method: Outcomes of first cycle of consultation* (2006/12), Bristol: HEFCE.

HEFCE (2006) *HEFCE Strategic Plan 2006–11* (2006/13), Bristol: HEFCE.

Leitch Review of Skills (2005) *Skills in the UK: The Long-term Challenge*, Interim Report, London: HMSO.

National Committee of Inquiry into Higher Education (NCIHE) (1997) *Higher Education in the Learning Society. Main Report*, London: NCIHE.

Parry, G. (2005) *The Higher Education Role of Further Education Colleges* Research Report to the *Review of the Future of Further Education Colleges* (the Foster Review), Appendix 8, London, DfES and LSC, London, 18 pp http://www.dfes.gov.uk/furthereducation/fereview/evidence.shtml

Parry, G. and Thompson, A. (2002) *Closer by Degrees: The past, present and future of higher education in further education colleges*, London: LSDA.

Parry, G., Davies, P. and Williams, J. (2003) *Dimensions of Difference: Higher education in the learning and skills sector*, London: LSDA.

Parry, G., Davies, P. and Williams, J. (2004) *Difference, Diversity and Distinctiveness: Higher education in the learning and skills sector*, London: LSDA.

QAA (2004a) *Foundation Degree Qualification Benchmark*, Gloucester: QAA.

QAA (2004b) *Learning from Higher Education in Further Education Colleges in England*, Gloucester: QAA.

QAA (2005) *Learning from Reviews of Foundation Degrees in England Carried Out in 2004–05*, Gloucester: QAA.

QAA (2005) *Report of a Survey to Follow Up Foundation Degree Reviews Carried Out in 2002–03*, Gloucester: QAA.

QAA (2005) *Report of a Survey of Foundation Degrees Converted from Existing Higher National Diplomas since 2001*, Gloucester: QAA.

QAA (2006) *Learning from Higher Education in Further Education Colleges in England 2003–05*, Gloucester: QAA.

Index

The Index does not include key terms which are central to the content of the book: higher education, further education, HE and FE sectors, higher-level, partnership, collaboration, progression, widening participation, direct and indirect funding, franchise, consortium, mission, strategy, posts and roles – including HE coordinator and programme leader – and all types of higher level qualification. However, the complexity and differential usage of several of these terms are addressed in pages 25–30 and in appendix A. Page or chapter references in bold indicate that the term is the subject of that section or an entry in appendix C.